Workbook for Culinary Arts Management

Workbook, Videos and Practice Exam

—— Second Edition ——

T0320997

Written by **Dominic Hawkes** and **Daniel John Stine**

SDC
PUBLICATIONS

SDC Publications

P.O. Box 1334

Mission, KS 66222

913-262-2664

www.SDCpublications.com

Publisher: Stephen Schroff

The author and publisher of this book have used their best efforts in preparing this book. These efforts include the development, research and testing of the material presented. The author and publisher shall not be liable in any event for incidental or consequential damages with, or arising out of, the furnishing, performance, or use of the material.

ISBN-10	1-63057-618-2
ISBN-13	978-1-63057-618-9

Printed and bound in the United States of America.

Intended Audience

Created for students in a culinary arts program, this workbook covers the wide range of food-related topics and provides weekly hands-on exercises and worksheets. At the conclusion of this course students will be prepared to take the ServSafe® Food Protection Manager certification exam.

Errata

Please check the publisher's website from time to time for any errors or typos found once printed. Simply browse to *www.SDCpublications.com*, and then navigate to the page for this book. Click the **View/Submit Errata** link in the upper right corner of the page. If you find an error, please submit it so we can correct it in the next edition. You may contact the publisher with comments or suggestions at *service@SDCpublications.com*.

Introduction

This workbook provides a collection of study materials to both learn about culinary arts and to prepare for the ServSafe® Food Protection Manager certification exam. With a range of options for most learning styles, this book will help improve your skill level and provide an additional boost of confidence, which is sure to increase the chances of a successful exam outcome. Study material for all learning styles provided, including:

Printed Coursebook

- Introduction to culinary arts *no previous experience required*
- Focused Study *on certification objective domains*
- Chapter summary *helpful study material*
- Glossary reference *orange text means that word is defined in the glossary*
- Food Code section reference *in margins supports further exploration of a topic*

Printed Student Workbook

- Personal copy *students can write in*
- Weekly exercises *supporting a full semester*
- Exercise-specific supporting video *featuring all necessary steps*
- Recipe worksheets *for each exercise*
- Forms and schedules *such as food cost worksheet & equipment lists*
- Flashcards *cut out with scissors*

Downloads

- Videos *with optional captioning*
- Practice Software *90 timed questions like the official exam*
- Downloads *accessible with code found in Student Workbook*

Chapter Organization

- Recipe and chapter video
- 5 sections with reading assignments
- Activites, Worksheets, & Questions
- Grading rubrics

Practice Exam

This Student Workbook concludes with an overview of the included practice exam software download. This software mimics the real exam as much as possible, in terms of user interface, number and types of questions, as well as a time constraint. While this study guide cannot claim to cover every possible question that may arise in the exam, it does help to firm up your basic knowledge to positively deal with most questions... thus, leaving more time to reflect on the more difficult questions.

About the Authors

Dominic Hawkes is a Master Chef of Great Britain with over 29 years of experience in the food service industry. He began his culinary journey in London's finest hotels, including the Ritz, Radisson Edwardian & Prince Regent, and the Dubai International Aerospace Show. With a diploma in culinary arts, food hygiene, and certification in nutrition & health, and wines & spirits, Dominic later completed a bachelor's degree in business studies, majoring in hospitality studies.

After working for Bank of America's Corporate Food Services, Dominic became the Food & Beverage Director at Charlotte City Club, where he worked for 19 years before transitioning into teaching Culinary Arts. Since 2019, he has been teaching at the Lancaster County School District Career Center in South Carolina, where he is certified to teach and proctor four certifications by the National Restaurant Association, including ProStart Culinary & ServSafe.

Dominic's commitment to education is exemplified by his successful efforts in 2022 when he and the Lancaster County School District Career Center became the first secondary school in the Carolinas to receive American Culinary Federation accreditation, certifying students with the coveted Certified Fundamentals Cook (CFC) designation.

2020-21	2022-23	2022-23	2022-23
South Carolina ACTE New Teacher of the Year	South Carolina ACTE FYI New Teacher of the Year	South Carolina ACTE Culinary Award	EEA Best Practice & Knowledge Sharing Award

Dominic's dedication to his students was further highlighted during the 2020 pandemic lockdowns when he swiftly adapted his classes to an online platform. Since then, he has shared his valuable insights with audiences worldwide through his popular YouTube channel, Chef Hawkes. His tireless efforts in the culinary arts also earned him multiple accolades at the state and national levels, including his victory at the Carolina Classic Cook-Off and being featured on PBS Charlotte (WTVI).

Dominic is happily married to his awesome art teacher wife Courtney of 20+ years and has two amazing children, Jack & Tate. (Who followed different paths in Career & Technical Education (CTE) in high school too.)

Daniel John Stine is a certified ServSafe® food protection manager and a Wisconsin registered architect with over twenty years of experience. Daniel works at Lake|Flato, a top-ranked architecture firm based in San Antonio, Texas, USA. He has worked on many multi-million-dollar projects, plus a nearly $1 billion dollar hospital project in the Midwest. Throughout these years of professional practice, Stine has worked on many food service-related projects with commercial kitchens which require careful attention to the flow of food and food-related design codes and State/City/County health department regulations. He has also worked in multiple roles in the foodservice industry, including line and prep cook, dishwasher, server, and host.

He is a member of the American Institute of Architects (AIA), and the Illumination Engineering Society (IES), and serves on a national AIA Committee on the Environment (COTE) Leadership Group and was a co-author of the AIA Climate Action Business Playbook. Dan is also the chair of a national IES committee.

Daniel has 20 years of academic experience. Committed to furthering the design profession, Stine teaches interior design and graduate architecture students at North Dakota State University (NDSU) and has lectured for design programs at Penn State, Pratt Institute, Prairie View A&M, Northern Iowa State, University of Minnesota, & University of Texas at San Antonio (UTSA). As an adjunct instructor, Dan taught for twelve years at Lake Superior College in Minnesota. He has presented internationally on architecture and design technology.

With 20 years of experience developing content for the academic market, Stine has written 17 textbooks. These books are used in high schools, technical colleges, and universities across North America. His book *Residential Design Using Autodesk Revit* is the #1 Revit book in the academic market in North America. Five of Stine's books are focused on helping students become certified on various topics, including:

Student Workbook

Table of Contents

The chapters in this workbook align with the chapters in the coursebook.

Videos

Each chapter includes a video covering the recipe and relevant topics from the coursebook chapter. Videos include:

- Food safety topics
- Culinary arts
- Food Safety Manager certification topics
- Review of example exam questions

Practice Exam Software

This workbook includes access to the practice example software covered in chapter 15w. The practice exam includes the following features:

- Timed – 90 minutes
- Graded – 70% passing
- 90 Sample questions
- Unlimited attempts

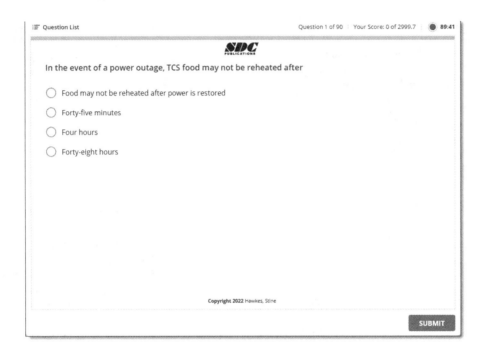

Study Material

Additional study material included when studying for the manager certification:

- Certification exam study guide (chapter 16w)
- Flash cards
- Practice exam software
- Videos

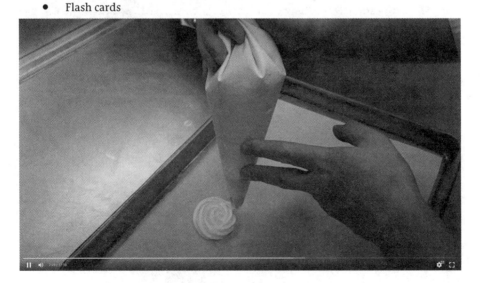

Chapter 1W

A World of Food

Every culture is defined by several things, such as its institutions, form of government, arts, customs, and even its food! While food is necessary to maintain life, it also can invigorate life and bring people together. When you think of weddings, births, promotions, and even the death of loved ones, people often gather around food — not just because it is necessary, but because it can be comforting or perhaps reminds us of "the old days". The multitude of things that happen to bring this food to our fingertips is the exciting adventure you are about to embark on in this exploration of the culinary arts!

Key Terms

Keep an eye out for these essential topics in the coursebook:

- Culture
- Restaurant
- Full-time (FTE)
- Part-time (PTE)
- Roles
- Skills
- Front-of-house
- Back-of-house

Objectives

After working through this chapter in the coursebook, you should be able to explain the following to friends and family:

- Appreciate the community value
- Explain the history of restaurants
- Learn about a career in food
- Describe the various roles
- Explain the front-of-house
- Describe the back-of-house

Section 1

Reading assignment:

Read pages 1-8 in the coursebook, and then complete the activities below.

Fill in the missing words:

In ancient Rome, before being buried in volcanic ash by the eruption of Mt. Vesuvius in 79 A.D., Pompeii and Herculaneum had _____ _____ (aka Thermopolium). Locals could purchase hot, _____ food on the side of the street. Consider how elements of this can be seen today in _____ _____, counter service at an amusement park, or (although mobile) a food truck.

Questions:

What is the value to the customer in visiting a restaurant?

    a)   Time saved
    b)   No skills required
    c)   No cleanup after the meal
    d)   All of the above

What is meant by an agrarian lifestyle?

    a.   An affluent population, who require restaurants or servants for sustenance.
    b.   A single settled location where the population work the land for food.
    c.   The population constantly moves to find food and appropriate shelter to survive.
    d.   A modern understanding of utilizing technology like microwaves to make eating more efficient.

In early 1600s America, what type of conditions were present, if you traveled and wanted to get a meal?

    a.   Stop at the regular rest stops on the highways.
    b.   Make friends with the locals to find the best restaurant in town that served the best steaks.
    c.   Go to the town inn at the specified mealtime to enjoy the single choice meal available.
    d.   Make sure to place your request for food early in the day, to get any special dietary requests confirmed.

What is the long-term trend, when we look at the population eating at home or eating away from home?

    a.   They are about the same levels as each other.
    b.   Eating at home will continue to rise for the foreseeable future.
    c.   Eating out will continue to rise for the foreseeable future.
    d.   Eating will become a thing of the past.

Who is your idol? (Individual assignment)

Think about all the people who have inspired you in some way, to bring you to this class. The hospitality world is full of very hard-working individuals, who will all tell you that hard work, knowledge and a little luck is what brought them success. Take some time to research one individual who brings you inspiration. This individual may be someone who is a celebrity and still alive today, someone who lived a long time ago and still influences the industry or someone personally in your life—maybe a friend or family member. Research this individual using the internet, books or magazines and write a short paper to present to your class this week. If your teacher has an available screen, consider sharing images that could offer visuals on the individual. Your presentation should be no longer than 5 minutes.

Section 2

Reading Assignment:

Read pages 8-21 in the coursebook, and then complete the activities below.

Fill in the missing words:

Many people work for companies that provide food-related services to restaurants, cafeterias, and catering services. The _____ companies offer products, such as raw _____ and condiments. Other examples include sales representatives for distributors and products, kitchen _____ repair personnel, and marketing/graphic design professionals.

Questions:

Which of the following positions would we class as a background or "back of house" employee?

   a)   Host
   b)   Cook
   c)   Food Service Manager
   d)   Bartender

What is one of the most important roles for a host?

   a)   Serve food rapidly.
   b)   Assist the bartender with drinks when servers are busy.
   c)   Seat tables in a balanced way, to not overload service sections.
   d)   Be available to the service team to assist with bussing at busy times.

In a large, sophisticated kitchen brigade, the pantry chef is in charge of all the cold preparations, like salads. What is the French term for this position?

   a)   Poissonier
   b)   Garde Manger
   c)   Sous Chef
   d)   Patissier

In the foodservice industry, communication skills are essential, in both the front and back of house. What term do we give to the essential part of receiving communications?

   a)   Certified listening
   b)   Essential listening
   c)   Active talking
   d)   Active listening

Who is your idol? (Individual assignment)

Continue researching your idol from the hospitality world. Prepare to make a presentation and have some visuals to accompany your presentation.

Section 3

Activity:

- Your instructor will take you on a tour of the kitchen. Today we will look at the **large foodservice equipment** like ovens, salamander, food mixers, etc. Take some time to write below the names of the pieces of equipment and a very brief description of their use.

Equipment name:	Purpose:
Example: Oven	Baking, roasting & braising.

Who is your idol? (Individual assignment)

Continue researching your idol from the hospitality world. Prepare to make a presentation and have some visuals to accompany your presentation. You should have this completed for the next class. Share any visuals you plan to use in your presentation with your instructor.

Section 4

Activity:

- Your instructor will take you on a tour of the kitchen. Today we will look at the **smallwares and kitchen knives** like chef knives, peelers, zesters, rolling pins, portion scoops, etc. Take some time to write below the names of the pieces of equipment and a very brief description of their use.

Equipment name:	Purpose:
Example: Zester	Peel the zest of citrus fruits for use in recipes.

Who is your idol? (Individual assignment)

Each student will make a presentation of no more than 5 minutes on their hospitality world idol they chose. Follow the rubric to maximize your grade. (There will be time in this class and the next to complete all the presentations.)

Section 5

Activity:

- Your instructor will finish the kitchen tour with the rules of how the kitchen will operate. Your instructor is the Executive Chef of the kitchen and has the final decision on your entry to the kitchen. It is a privilege to work in a well-equipped environment with dangerous equipment. All rules surrounding personal and food safety must be followed. Your success depends on your attitude and work ethic to the kitchen, instructor, fellow students and the food.

- Enter the rules of your kitchen below:

Kitchen rules:

Correct Attire (*What to wear and not wear*):

Who is your idol? (Individual assignment)

Each student will make a presentation of no more than 5 minutes on their hospitality world idol they chose. Follow the rubric to maximize your grade.

Grading Rubric – Who is Your Idol Presentation?

Students will choose an idol from the past or present who has inspired them to enter into the hospitality industry. They will research using all available information and create a presentation of no more than 5 minutes. Visual aids strongly improve the presentation and are recommended.

Students will be offered adequate time to complete this task, with scrutiny on their written information, accuracy, attractiveness and the quality of their finished product.

It is recommended that students keep the information clear and easy to present to the class.

Culinary Arts

Who is Your Idol Presentation Rubric

Student name _____   Date _____

Category	Specifications	Highly Skilled (Professional) 25 pts	Skilled (First Cook) 20 pts	Moderately Skilled (Commis) 15pts	Low Skilled 10pts (Developing)	No Attempt 0pts	Comments
Accuracy with researching the idol (25pts Max)	Reading, comprehending & creating the presentation with accuracy	No guidance needed with reading, comprehending & creating the presentation with accuracy	Minimal guidance needed with reading, comprehending & creating the presentation with accuracy	Some guidance needed with reading, comprehending & creating the presentation with accuracy	Substantial guidance needed with reading, comprehending & creating the presentation with accuracy	No attempt made	
Written information (25pts Max)	Quality of written information to prepare for the presentation	Exemplary standards maintained with no guidance	Very good standards maintained with some guidance	Good standards maintained, needed guidance	Poor standards maintained, needed guidance	No attempt made	
Attractiveness of the presentation (25pts Max)	Accompanying images offered to enhance the presentation.	Excellent quality with no guidance	Very good quality with some guidance	Good quality with guidance needed	Poor quality with guidance needed	No attempt made	
Quality of finished product (25pts Max)	Final appearance of prepared presentation with quality work achieved.	Excellent quality finished presentation, well presented.	Very good quality finished presentation, well presented.	Good quality finished presentation, well presented.	Poor quality finished presentation.	No attempt made	

Grading Rubric – Kitchen Tour Record

Students will be given a full tour of the kitchen to learn or refresh their memories on where the large foodservice equipment as well as the knives and smallwares are stored and how they are operated and maintained. Students will also learn or be refreshed on the rules of operating a safe, professional kitchen, including the attitude you show towards the equipment, people and food. Understanding these factors will ensure your success in the hospitality world.

Culinary Arts
Kitchen Tour Record Rubric

Student name _____   Date _____

Category	Specifications	Highly Skilled (Professional) 25 pts	Skilled (First Cook) 20 pts	Moderately Skilled (Commis) 15pts	Low Skilled 10pts (Developing)	No Attempt 0pts	Comments
Written information 25pts	All written information is correct and spelled correctly.	No guidance needed, with all written information being accurate	Minimal guidance needed with all written information being accurate	Some guidance needed with all written information being accurate	Substantial guidance needed with all written information being accurate	No attempt made	
Safety & Sanitation 25pts	Correct information regarding regulatory authority rules are entered.	Exemplary standards maintained with no guidance	Very good standards maintained with some guidance	Good standards maintained, needed guidance	Poor standards maintained, needed guidance	No attempt made	
Accuracy of overall documentation 25pts	Quality & precision of work.	Excellent precision with no guidance	Very good precision with some guidance	Good precision with guidance needed	Poor precision with guidance needed	No attempt made	
Quality of finished product 25pts	Prepared work with quality achieved and detail required to show retention.	Excellent quality finished record, well presented	Very good quality finished record, well presented	Good quality finished record	Poor quality finished record	No attempt made	

Chapter Summary

Even if you still don't see a career in the foodservice industry for yourself after working through this chapter, or the entire book, you will have a better appreciation for all involved in the process. From the facilities and equipment to the acquisition and storage, as well as cooking and serving, there are a lot of moving parts. All of these must be managed carefully to protect the customer, the reputation of the operation, and let's not forget the time-honored tradition that has helped shape community and family traditions and even define many cultures.

- The coffee shop, café, and restaurant have deep roots in Western civilization dating back to the 1600s. Gathering around food is a time-honored tradition all around the world.

- A career in the foodservice industry can be rewarding and lead to unexpected opportunities and places in the world.

- Food employees must have good customer skills, including good communication skills.

- The fast-moving environment often requires physical strength and stamina.

- Workers with disabilities have certain rights afforded by the Americans with Disabilities Act (ADA).

- Supporting safety and efficiency, the foodservice industry has specific terms for staff roles, spaces within the operation, and equipment.

[Blank Page]

Chapter 2W

Handling Food Safely

Much of what the chapter in the coursebook covers will sound like common sense and might be what many people already do at home when cooking. However, given the fast-paced restaurant environment and the potential dangers to consumers, especially the **highly susceptible population** (HSP) or those with allergies, safe food handling best practices in the foodservice industry cannot be left to chance.

The United States (U.S.) **Food and Drug Administration** (FDA) created and maintains the **Food Code**, which they recommend state and local jurisdictions adopt to protect food employees and the public from physical and foodborne illness dangers. Every food employee must thoroughly understand safe food handling through training, practice, enforcement, and consistent **corrective action**. By doing so, everyone will work as a team, and muscle memory will kick in when things get busy or distracting.

Key Terms

Keep an eye out for these essential topics in the coursebook:

- Highly Susceptible Population (HSP)
- Personal Hygiene
- Corrective Action
- Carrier
- Ready-to-eat Foods (RTE)
- Handwashing
- Protective coverings
- Restrict and Exclude

Objectives

After working through this chapter in the coursebook, you should be able to explain the following to friends and family:

- Understand the importance of personal hygiene
- Know how and when to wash hands
- Describe ready-to-eat foods (RTE)
- The importance of single-use gloves
- Explain the difference between exclude and restrict
- Know when to report health-related issues

Recipe

Recipe: Chef's Salad

A chef's salad is a traditional American salad made of lettuce leaves, cheese, meats, boiled egg, tomatoes, cucumber, and other seasonal vegetables. It can be served tossed or composed with the customer's choice of dressing.

Ingredients:

- 2 eggs
- 3oz bacon
- 1/2 cup extra virgin olive oil
- 1/4 cup balsamic vinegar (or another preferred vinegar)
- Salt & pepper to taste
- 4oz sliced turkey
- 4oz mozzarella
- 1/2 head romaine lettuce
- 2 green onions
- 6 radishes
- 1 tomato
- 4oz English cucumber

All topping items can be substituted to preference or seasonality.

Section 1

Reading assignment:

Read pages 25-33 in the coursebook, and then complete the activities below.

Fill in the missing words:

Jewelry is prohibited while preparing food, except for a simple _____ _____.

This includes _____ information jewelry on the arms, such as a bracelet. It is difficult to clean

around jewelry properly, and it is _____ to lose it in the food and possibly harm a consumer.

Questions:

Smoking, vaping, chewing gum, or tobacco is prohibited except?

    a) In the staff parking lot
    b) In designated areas
    c) In the staff break room
    d) On weekends

When is it NOT necessary to wash your hands?

    a. When entering a food preparation area.
    b. Before putting on clean, single-use gloves for working with food.
    c. When continuing to prep the same ingredients.
    d. Between glove changes.

When washing your hands, what is important that happens when you shut off the water?

    a. Completely shut the water off to not waste the resource.
    b. Make sure the hand sink has all splashes wiped up.
    c. Tell the manager if the tap is stiff.
    d. Turn the tap off with a paper towel, to prevent contamination of your clean hands.

Fill in the blank: An essential rule is to never handle _____ foods with bare hands.

    a. Ready-to-eat
    b. Chicken & Poultry
    c. Dirty root vegetables
    d. Raw fish

Create a Handwashing Poster

Design your own hand washing chart with your new knowledge and the assistance of the example below. Ensure all wording is correct and easily legible. Keep designs simple and add some color, if available. Read the rubric to achieve the best grade.

Use the following page to create your poster, which may be removed from the workbook.

1 Rinse under clean, warm running water.

2 Apply soap.

3 Rub all surfaces of the hands and fingernails together vigorously for at least 10 to 15 seconds.

4 Rinse thoroughly with clean, warm running water.

5 Thoroughly dry the hands and exposed portions of arms.

Handwashing Poster

Name:_____ Date: _____

[Blank Page]

Section 2

Reading Assignment:

Read pages 33-37 in the coursebook, and then complete the activities below.

Fill in the missing words:

To keep hair from touching or contaminating food, the _____ _____ requires that food employees wear hair restraints, such as _____, hats, and clothing covering body hair. This requirement does not apply to staff who only serve _____ and packaged or wrapped foods. Servers, hosts, and bus staff are also excluded from covering hair if they present minimal risk of contaminating exposed food, equipment, or utensils.

Questions:

Which of the following is NOT a beverage rule for food production staff:

    a. Closed container; *with lid and straw or sip lid*
    b. Stored on a non-food contact surface; *e.g., a supply shelf or atop a microwave*
    c. Separate from exposed food, clean equipment, or unwrapped single-use articles
    d. The cup must have a retractable straw

Food workers are not allowed to eat meals in or around food preparation or production areas. Instead, they must eat in which of the following?

    a. Dining room
    b. Staff breakroom
    c. Quiet corner of the kitchen
    d. Outside of the operation

Which of the following symptoms do NOT have to be reported?

    a. Vomiting
    b. Migraine
    c. Diarrhea
    d. Sore throat with fever
    e. Jaundice
    f. Infected cuts, wounds, or lesions containing pus on exposed body parts

Who is not considered part of the High-Risk Population?

    a. Preschool-aged children
    b. Pregnant women
    c. Elderly adults
    d. Anyone with immune health conditions

Complete your hand washing chart and submit it for a vote with the class. The best charts can be displayed near the hand washing sinks in the kitchen.

Section 3

Read the chef's salad recipe carefully and list all known Time & Temperature Control for Safety (TCS) ingredients.

Video Assignment:

Watch the chef's salad video carefully and note any new skills needed.

Activity:

- With your team, document new areas of food hygiene risk you have learned from the video content.

In the Kitchen:

- In the kitchen, measure & weigh the raw ingredients for your team's chef's salad.
- Cook and chill any ingredients that require this preparation.
- Wrap and label all ingredients.
- Create and record your equipment mise en place list with your team to be ready for tomorrow's lab.

Section 4

Prepare the chef's salad with a team. Read the grading rubric to achieve the maximum points available.

In the Kitchen:

Each team creates their mise en place for each individual ingredient for the chef's salad. (Preparation of ingredients & equipment needed.)

The team will follow the recipe, making any needed alterations to the seasonally available items. Create the salad with any assistance needed from the instructor or the preparation video.

Each team should wash, rinse & sanitize their equipment and work surfaces, to the standards shown in the video and discussed in the textbook.

Section 5

Individual presentation:

Each team will be given ten minutes to prepare a two-minute presentation for the rest of the class.

- Students should concentrate on their successes and challenges and they should report if they have an item of improvement for the next time they repeat the recipe.

Watch and participate in the end-of-chapter review video.

Recipe Cost Sheet:

Your instructor will begin to assist you in filling out the recipe costing sheet. The first version has step-by-step instructions for you to follow.

Once completed, students should work out the recipe cost and then complete the per-portion price. In future chapters, students will take the lead in completing "costing sheets" for projects they complete.

Recipe Cost Worksheet

Menu Item				
Number of Portions		**Portion Size**		

A	B	C	D	E	F
Ingredient	Purchase Unit	Purchase cost	Unit cost	Amount Needed	Ingredient Cost
Example: **Butter**	**454g**	**$4.56**	**$0.01/1g**	**280g**	**$2.80**
					'
Example: **Butter**	**1lb**	**$4.56**	**$ 0.285 /oz**	**10oz**	**$2.785**

Total recipe cost		G
Number of portions from recipe		H
Portion Cost		I

Some helpful conversions:

- 16oz = 1lb
- 8floz = 1 cup
- 2 cups = 1pt
- 2pts = 1qt
- 4qt = 1 Gal
- 3tsp = 1 tbsp.
- 1000g = 1kg
- 1000ml = 1L

Step 1: Fill out each ingredient name in column A and the name of the recipe.

Step 2: Fill column B with the unit amount purchased from the store. This must match or be converted to the recipe measurements Lbs., kg, pts., etc.

Step 3: Column C is the cost of the purchase unit from column B.

Step 4: Column D breaks your measurement units down to a singular unit, 1oz./ 1g/ 1floz etc.

Step 5: Column D calculation C ÷ B = D

Step 6: Column E, enter the recipe required amount.

Step 7: D x E = F

Step 8: Add all lines in column F to give the total recipe cost in line G.

Step 9: Add to line H the number of portions created, when making the recipe in the kitchen.

Step 10: $G \div H = I$, giving you the portion cost.

Recipe Cost Worksheet

Name:_____ Date: _____

Menu Item	
Number of Portions	**Portion Size**

Ingredient	Purchase Unit	Purchase cost	Unit cost	Amount Needed	Ingredient Cost

Total recipe cost	
Number of portions from recipe	
Portion Cost	

[Blank Page]

Grading Rubric - Hand Washing Poster

Students will see examples and professionally and accurately replicate the six requirements for correctly washing hands.

Students will be offered adequate time to complete this task, with scrutiny on their written information, safety and sanitation, accuracy, attractiveness and the quality of their finished product.

It is recommended that students use simple drawn examples to keep the information clear. Add some color to your work, as a bold poster is eye appealing and will be more successful in educating others when on display.

Safety and accuracy are key to your success.

Culinary Arts
Hand Washing Poster

Student name _____ Date _____

Category	Specifications	Highly Skilled (Professional) 25 pts	Skilled (First Cook) 20 pts	Moderately Skilled (Commis) 15pts	Low Skilled 10pts (Developing)	No Attempt 0pts	Comments
Written information 25pts	All written information is spelled correctly and is accurate	No guidance needed with all written information being accurate	Minimal guidance needed with all written information being accurate	Some guidance needed with all written information being accurate	Substantial guidance needed with all written information being accurate	No attempt made	
Safety & Sanitation 25pts	Correct information according to regulatory rules is presented	Exemplary standards maintained with no guidance	Very good standards maintained with some guidance	Good standards maintained, needed guidance	Poor standards maintained, needed guidance	No attempt made	
Accuracy of overall poster 25pts	Quality & precision of work, with accuracy of images and overall poster	Excellent precision with no guidance	Very good precision with some guidance	Good precision with guidance needed	Poor precision with guidance needed	No attempt made	
Quality of finished product 25pts	Final appearance of prepared poster with quality work achieved	Excellent quality finished poster, well presented	Very good quality finished poster, well presented	Good quality finished poster	Poor quality finished products	No attempt made	

Grading Rubric - Chef's Salad

Students will see the video example, safely, professionally and accurately replicating the dish.

Students will be offered adequate time to complete this task, with scrutiny on their safety and sanitation, accuracy, attractiveness and the quality of their finished product.

Students should ensure all equipment and work surfaces are cleaned, sanitized, and stored.

Safety and accuracy are key to your success.

Culinary Arts
Chef's Salad Recipe Rubric

Student name _____   Date _____

Category	Specifications	Highly Skilled (Professional) 25 pts	Skilled (First Cook) 20 pts	Moderately Skilled (Commis) 15pts	Low Skilled 10pts (Developing)	No Attempt 0pts	Comments
Accuracy reading & following the recipe (25pts Max)	Reading, comprehending & following the recipe is done with accuracy	No guidance needed with reading, comprehending & following the recipe.	Minimal guidance needed with reading, comprehending & following the recipe.	Some guidance needed with reading, comprehending & following the recipe	Substantial guidance needed with reading, comprehending & following the recipe	No attempt made	
Safety & Sanitation (25pts Max)	Correctly following all regulatory authority rules when preparing foods.	Exemplary standards maintained with no guidance	Very good standards maintained with some guidance	Good standards maintained, needed guidance	Poor standards maintained, needed guidance	No attempt made	
Accuracy & precision of preparations (25pts Max)	Accuracy & precision of work, with knife cuts & preparations.	Excellent precision with no guidance	Very good precision with some guidance	Good precision with guidance needed	Poor precision with guidance needed	No attempt made	
Quality of finished product (25pts Max)	Final appearance of prepared Chef Salad with quality work achieved.	Excellent quality finished salad, well presented.	Very good quality finished salad, well presented.	Good quality finished salad.	Poor quality finished product.	No attempt made	

Chapter Summary

The theme of this chapter is how food employees can keep food safe from contamination. The main goal of safe food handling is to protect the *consumer* from foodborne illnesses caused by contaminated food. This is especially true for the highly susceptible population (HSP), who are more likely to experience foodborne illness and have a more severe, potentially fatal reaction due to their age or underlying health conditions. The preventative measures discussed in this chapter include maintaining good personal hygiene, properly washing hands, using protective coverings as required, and reporting any personal health issues. With proper training, monitoring, corrective action, and retraining, a food establishment significantly reduces the risks of a foodborne illness outbreak.

- The highly susceptible population (HSP) have a higher risk of experiencing foodborne illness due to age and health.
- Staff must arrive to work clean, well-groomed, and practice good personal hygiene.
- Corrective action involves intervening in an unsafe practice and retraining.
- A food handler is considered a carrier when they have a virus or disease that can spread through food.
- Ready-to-eat foods (RTE) can be eaten as-is and do not require subsequent or additional cooking. RTE examples include lettuce, bread, potato chips, and cake.
- Food employees must know how and when to wash their hands to reduce the chances of cross-contamination.
- Bright-colored bandages & single-use gloves must be used to avoid food contamination.
- Exclusion means a food employee is not allowed to enter or work in a food establishment, whereas restriction limits them from working with clean equipment or exposed food.

When these symptoms occur before arriving to work, staff must not report to work. Instead, they are to call or text their manager. When these symptoms are reported or observed during a shift, the manager will **exclude** or **restrict** the employee following the FDA Decision Tree.

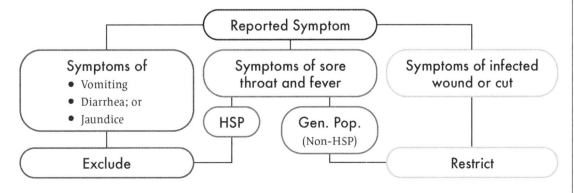

[Blank Page]

Chapter 3W

Bad Bugs

The world is filled with microorganisms, many of which are helpful to our health and the complex ecosystem surrounding us. However, some "bad bugs" (or pathogens) are harmful to human health and need to be avoided or managed and kept to safe levels. Good personal hygiene, covered in the previous chapter, is how people protect themselves from getting sick from bad bugs, such as washing hands often (especially after using the toilet), wearing clean clothes, and personal grooming.

In the foodservice industry, understanding and managing "bad bugs" is a serious matter since the health of others, i.e., the consumer or the public, is at stake. There are many ways dangerous pathogens can enter food and cause foodborne illness when consumed. For example, food can arrive contaminated, it can become contaminated by poor food handling, and it can become contaminated by food employees who are sick while they work or do not practice good personal hygiene. Proper training and application paired with consistent corrective action are crucial to preventing foodborne illness or an outbreak involving two or more people.

Key Terms
Keep an eye out for these essential topics:

- Pathogens
- Bacteria
- FAT TOM
- Virus
- Spore
- Toxins
- Parasite
- Fungi

Objectives
After working through this chapter, you should be able to explain the following to friends and family:

- Describe the Big 6 pathogens
- Know the living pathogens: bacteria, fungi, and parasites
- Know the non-living entities: viruses, spores, and toxins
- Understand how FAT TOM relates to bacterial growth
- Explain the symptoms associated with the Big 6
- Know that some pathogens cannot be destroyed by cooking

Recipe

Recipe: American meringue cookies & Vacherin

The American meringue method is the simplest preparation with great results. There are also Swiss and Italian methods which take a lot more measurements, control, and experience to make. This reliable recipe will produce light, fluffy meringue cookies and nests (called Vacherin in French). In this recipe, we will cook the meringue at a relatively low temperature, so it remains a pure white color. This can then be garnished with fresh fruit, cream, ice cream, buttercream, and coulis sauces. Perfect for simple but beautiful desserts.

Ingredients:

- 360g white sugar
- 180g egg white
- 1.23ml cream of tartar
- optional filling ingredients

Section 1

Reading assignment:

Read pages 41-49 in the coursebook, and then complete the activities below.

Fill in the missing words:

F _____

A _____

T _____

T _____

O _____

M _____

Questions:

What are Pathogens?

    a)   Yeast cells used in cheese making.

    b)   Microorganisms which can cause foodborne illness.

    c)   Dangerous chemicals which can make foods toxic.

    d)   The name given to physical contaminants found in foods.

Which of the following are part of the BIG 6 Pathogens?

    a.   Clostridium Botulinum

    b.   Norovirus

    c.   Shiga toxin-producing Escherichia coli

    d.   Bacillus Cereus

What is the optimum temperature range for bacterial growth?

    e.   41°F – 135°F (5°C – 57°C)

    f.   0°F – 41°F (-18°C – 5°C)

    g.   32°F – 41°F (0°C – 5°C)

    h.   70°F – 125°F (21°C – 52°C)

Natural toxins are NOT found in…

    a.   Mushrooms

    b.   Shellfish

    c.   Fish

    d.   Meat

Activity:

Design your own FATTOM chart with your new knowledge, the example below, or any further research you do. Ensure all wording is correct and easily legible. Keep designs simple and add some color, if available. Read the rubric to achieve the best grade.

Use the following page to create your poster, which may be removed from the workbook.

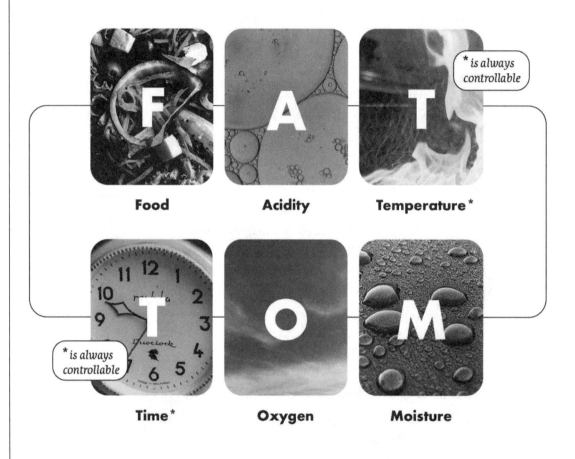

FATTOM Poster

Name_____ Date_____

[Blank Page]

Section 2

Reading Assignment:

Read pages 50-59 in the coursebook, and then complete the activities below.

Fill in the missing words:

The symptoms from some of the deadliest _____ can be delayed for hours, days, or even weeks. By the time symptoms occur, there can be severe organ damage. The most severe cases of psilocybin poisoning, _____ that cause neurological problems, occur in small children, where large doses can cause fever, hallucinations, and _____.

Questions:

Mold can survive in many environmental situations that some bacteria would struggle with. Which of the following are true?

    a.   PH range: 1-5.

    b.   50°F − 95°F (10°C − 35°C).

    c.   0.85 a_W or lower.

    d.   On smooth plastics.

Molds are made up of how many cells?

    a.   1

    b.   2

    c.   4

    d.   Many

Which of the following are true of a parasite?

    a.   They derive protection and nourishment from a host.

    b.   They thrive in meats & starchy foods.

    c.   Parasites do not grow in food but can be transmitted through it.

    d.   Parasites are not visible to the naked eye.

Where do viruses multiply?

    a.   Foods higher in vitamins

    b.   Foods high in protein

    c.   Non-potable water

    d.   In a host

Activity:

Complete your FATTOM poster and submit for a vote with the class. The best posters can be displayed in the kitchen or classroom.

Section 3

Read the meringue & Vacherin recipe carefully and list all known Time & Temperature Control for Safety (TCS) ingredients.

Video Assignment:

Watch the meringue & Vacherin video carefully and note any new skills needed.

Activity:

With your team, identify which items on the FATTOM list that will change, to inhibit bacterial growth, as the meringues are prepared and cooked.

In the Kitchen:

- In the kitchen, measure & weigh the raw ingredients for your team's meringues.
- Wrap and label all ingredients and store them appropriately.
- Create and record your equipment mise en place list with your team to be ready for tomorrow's lab.

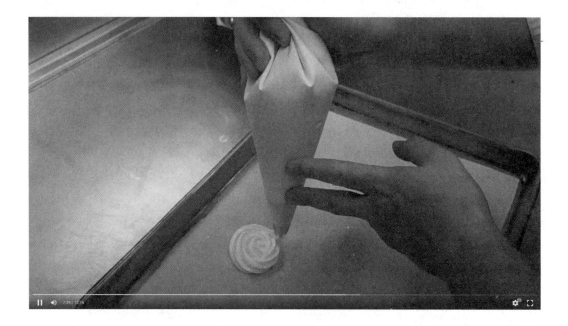

Section 4

Prepare the meringue cookies and Vacherin with a team. Bake them until they are cooked (possibly after your class is finished). Read the grading rubric to achieve the maximum points available.

In the Kitchen:

Each team creates their mise en place for the meringue (preparation of ingredients & equipment needed).

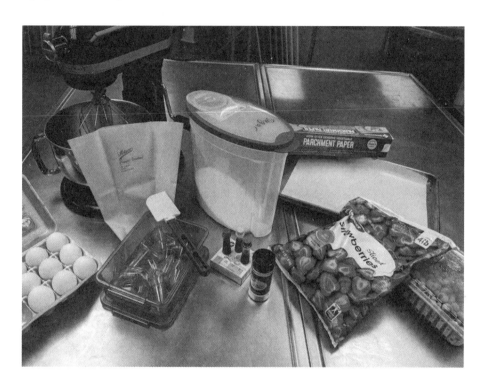

The team will follow the recipe, making any needed alterations to the seasonally available and chosen filling items. Create the meringue with any assistance needed from the instructor or the preparation video.

Each team should wash, rinse & sanitize their equipment and work surfaces, to the standards shown in the video and discussed in the textbook.

Section 5

Student presentation:

Each student will prepare their meringue with the available fillings and make a presentation to show the rest of the class.

Activity:

The students should state their successes with their completed meringue cookies or Vacherin and what they would choose to do to make an improvement next time.

Watch and participate in the end-of-chapter review video.

Grading Rubric - FATTOM Poster

Students will see examples and professionally and accurately replicate the FATTOM poster, using their knowledge. The format can vary from that of the example, but must contain the essential information.

Students will be offered adequate time to complete this task, with scrutiny on their written information, safety and sanitation, accuracy, attractiveness and the quality of their finished product.

It is recommended that students use simple drawn examples to keep the information clear. Add some color to your work, as a bold poster is eye appealing and will be more successful in educating others when on display.

Safety and accuracy are key to your success.

Culinary Arts
FATTOM Poster Rubric

Student name _____   Date _____

Category	Specifications	Highly Skilled (Professional) 25 pts	Skilled (First Cook) 20 pts	Moderately Skilled (Commis) 15pts	Low Skilled 10pts (Developing)	No Attempt 0pts	Comments
Written information 25pts	All written information is spelled correctly and is accurate	No guidance needed with all written information being accurate	Minimal guidance needed with all written information being accurate	Some guidance needed with all written information being accurate	Substantial guidance needed with all written information being accurate	No attempt made	
Safety & Sanitation 25pts	Correct information according to regulatory authority rules is presented	Exemplary standards maintained with no guidance	Very good standards maintained with some guidance	Good standards maintained, needed guidance	Poor standards maintained, needed guidance	No attempt made	
Accuracy of overall poster 25pts	Quality & precision of work, with accuracy of images and overall poster	Excellent precision with no guidance	Very good precision with some guidance	Good precision with guidance needed	Poor precision with guidance needed	No attempt made	
Quality of finished product 25pts	Final appearance of prepared poster with quality work achieved	Excellent quality finished poster, well presented	Very good quality finished poster, well presented	Good quality finished poster	Poor quality finished products	No attempt made	

Grading Rubric - Meringue Grading

Students will see the video example, safely, professionally and accurately replicating the dish.

Students will be offered adequate time to complete this task, with scrutiny on their safety and sanitation, accuracy, attractiveness and the quality of their finished product.

Students should ensure all equipment and work surfaces are cleaned, sanitized and stored.

Safety and accuracy are key to your success.

Culinary Arts
Meringue Recipe Rubric

Student name _____   Date _____

Category	Specifications	Highly Skilled (Professional) 25 pts	Skilled (First Cook) 20 pts	Moderately Skilled (Commis) 15pts	Low Skilled 10pts (Developing)	No Attempt 0pts	Comments
Accuracy reading & following the recipe (25pts Max)	Reading, comprehending & following the recipe is done with accuracy	No guidance needed with reading, comprehending & following the recipe.	Minimal guidance needed with reading, comprehending & following the recipe.	Some guidance needed with reading, comprehending & following the recipe	Substantial guidance needed with reading, comprehending & following the recipe	No attempt made	
Safety & Sanitation (25pts Max)	Correctly following all regulatory authority rules when preparing foods.	Exemplary standards maintained with no guidance	Very good standards maintained with some guidance	Good standards maintained, needed guidance	Poor standards maintained, needed guidance	No attempt made	
Accuracy & precision of preparations (25pts Max)	Accuracy & precision of work, with knife cuts & preparations.	Excellent precision with no guidance	Very good precision with some guidance	Good precision with guidance needed	Poor precision with guidance needed	No attempt made	
Quality of finished product (25pts Max)	Final appearance of prepared meringue dish with quality work achieved.	Excellent quality finished meringue dish, well presented.	Very good quality finished meringue dish, well presented.	Good quality finished meringue dish.	Poor quality finished product.	No attempt made	

Chapter Summary

As stated at the beginning of the chapter, understanding and managing "bad bugs" is a serious matter since the health of others, i.e., the consumer or the public, is at stake. There are many ways dangerous pathogens can enter food and cause foodborne illness when consumed. For example, food can arrive contaminated, it can become contaminated by poor food handling, and it can become contaminated by food employees who are sick while they work or do not practice good personal hygiene. Proper training and application paired with consistent corrective action are crucial to preventing foodborne illness or an outbreak involving two or more people.

- The Big 6 pathogens: Hepatitis A, Norovirus, Salmonella spp., Salmonella Typhi, Shiga toxin-producing Escherichia coli, Shigella spp.
- Living pathogens grow in the right conditions: bacteria, fungi, and parasites
- Know the non-living entities that appropriate cells of a host: viruses, spores, and toxins
- FAT TOM stands for: Food, Acidity, Temperature, Time, Oxygen, and Moisture
- The symptoms associated with various pathogens are listed in the previous section.
- Poisons cannot be destroyed or made inactive but cannot be destroyed by cooking.

There are four phases of bacterial growth: slow growth (lag-phase), rapid growth (log-phase), equilibrium (stationary-phase), and reduction (death-phase). Notice in the graph that rapid growth occurs within the temperature danger zone, where bacteria can double in as little as 20 minutes. Once food reaches its minimum internal temperature, bacteria begin to die quickly.

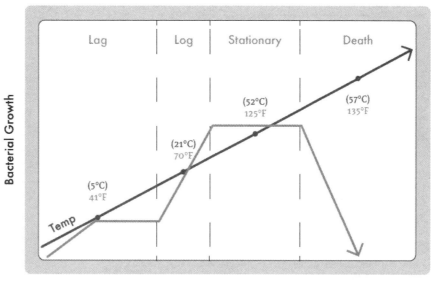

Time

Food

Like all living things, bacteria need a source of food such as proteins and carbohydrates (an intrinsic factor of food) to survive. Some foods support the growth of bacteria more than others, especially if the extrinsic factors of time and temperature are abused. These foods are referred to as TCS Foods (Time/Temperature Control for Safety Foods); examples are eggs, dairy products, and meats.

Acidity

The pH value of food, which is a measurement of acidity, is based on the following scale:

- 0.0 Highly acidic
- 7.0 Neutral
- 14.0 Highly alkaline

Bacterial growth is optimal in foods with little or no acidity (pH 7.5–4.6). Microbial growth is slowed when the pH is adjusted in either direction from this optimal range. For example, foods with high acidity or when used as an ingredient help limit bacterial growth (below 4.5 pH). Examples of foods with high acidity or low pH levels are:

- Limes: 1.8–2.4
- Vinegar: 2.0–3.4
- Cranberries: 2.3–2.5

Temperature

Like pH levels, temperature values for bacterial growth have a minimum and maximum range, outside of which growth is limited. This range, called the temperature danger zone, is 41°F–135°F (5°C–57°C). Bacterial growth potential is highest when food is between 70°F–125°F (21°C–52°C).

Time

Time is necessary for bacterial growth, especially within the temperature danger zone. If food is held at improper temperatures for enough time, bacteria can multiply to dangerous levels. Many foods require active cooling methods to cool quickly enough to limit the growth of bacteria that can lead to foodborne illness.

Oxygen

Bacterial growth usually requires oxygen, but not always. In canned goods containing contaminants, bacteria can grow in low oxygen conditions. Certain bacteria can grow without oxygen in cooked rice and time-temperature abused baked potatoes.

Moisture (a_w)

The moisture content in food can contribute to bacterial growth. However, we are most interested in Water Activity (a_w) levels, not moisture content, when considering food safety. Water Activity is measured on a scale of 0-1.0. A solution of pure water is 1.0 a_w, which decreases as other substances are added. Conditions are ideal for bacterial growth when at or above 0.85a_w. Some bacteria survive on low-moisture foods such as spices (e.g., black pepper, 0.4a_w) and infant baby powder.

Chapter 4W
Food Hazards

Reading each chapter of the coursebook by itself, you might think it is the most important chapter, given all the essential topics covered and the potential dangers to the consumer. However, food operations and the food itself are complicated, and the information found throughout this book must be understood and practiced concurrently to ensure food safety. This should not be discouraging, given it is accomplished every day worldwide. When these topics are tackled pragmatically, and in a way that builds upon itself, the results are a fulfilling and rewarding career, not to mention loyal and satisfied customers. Achieving that result is one of the goals of this book.

This chapter covers food hazards, including physical, chemical, and allergens; biological hazards were covered in the previous chapter. Preventing these foodborne contaminants involves understanding cross-contact, cross-contamination, and intentional contamination. When a manager creates and maintains food safety and food defense programs, the chances of consumers being harmed by foodborne illness are greatly reduced.

Key Terms
Keep an eye out for these essential topics:

- Allergens
- The Big 9
- Cross-contact
- Anaphylaxis
- Cross-contamination
- Adulterated food
- Food defense
- ALERT
- FIRST

Objectives
After working through this chapter, you should be able to explain the following to friends and family:

- Learn about the types of food contaminants
- Understand what cross-contamination is and how to prevent it
- Describe the flow of food
- Explain what TCS Foods are
- Understand the types of thermometers and their uses
- Know how to calibrate a bimetallic thermometer

Recipe

Recipe: World Class Chicken Stock

The base for some of the world's most popular soups and sauces comes from a high-quality stock. Stock is generally derived from a base of vegetables, fish, veal, beef, game, or chicken bones. Other bones, such as pork or lamb, aren't used as much due to the higher fat content or overpowering flavors that can occur. An outstanding stock's important aspects are developing excellent flavor, body, and maintaining clarity.

Ingredients:

- 8lb chicken bones (or other bones, if chosen)
- 2 gallons of cold potable water
- 1lb mirepoix (50% onions, 25% celery & 25% Carrots)
- aromatics (bouquet garni or sachet d'epices)

Section 1

Reading assignment:

Read pages 63-71 in the coursebook, and then complete the activities below.

Fill in the missing words:

The FDA Food Code requires that poisonous or toxic materials be stored so they cannot _____ food, equipment, utensils, linens, or single-use articles. _____ _____ includes separating chemicals by space (i.e., distance) or partition (i.e., a separate room). When separating by distance, the Food Code does not allow these materials to be stored _____ food or equipment.

Questions:

What are the common symptoms of chemical poisoning?

    a. Vomiting & diarrhea

    b. Hives and dry skin

    c. Headaches

    d. Prolonged fever

Which of the following could be considered chemicals?

    a. Plant toxins

    b. Sanitizers

    c. Yeast

    d. Pesticides

Which of the following are NOT physical hazards?

    a. Bandages

    b. Artificial fingernails

    c. Bacillus Cereus

    d. Glass

Which of the following is a naturally occurring chemical hazard?

    a. Fish toxin

    b. Polish

    c. Cleaners

    d. Sanitizers

Activity

Design your own "The Big 9" chart of the most common allergen foods with your new knowledge, and from any further research you do. Ensure all wording is correct and easily legible. See the example below, and remember to keep designs simple and add some color, if available. Read the rubric to achieve the best grade.

The Big 9 Poster

Name_____ Date_____

[Blank Page]

Section 2

Reading Assignment:

Read pages 71-83 in the coursebook, and then complete the activities below.

Fill in the missing words:

When taking food orders, servers should inquire about allergies. Suppose someone identifies themselves as having a food allergy. In that case, the server can take _____, which include pointing out _____ _____ in items ordered by others at the table and informing the kitchen to use extra caution. To do this, service staff must be _____ on the ingredients in each menu item. Finally, the allergen-free plates must be clearly _____ when the food is served.

Questions:

The Big 9 account for what percentage of food allergies and severe allergic reactions among people in the U.S.?

    a.   80%

    b.   85%

    c.   90%

    d.   95%

The FDA Food Code indicates what as being the best method to minimize allergen threats?

    a.   Cook foods to 165 Fahrenheit.

    b.   Clean & sanitize equipment.

    c.   Season heavily with salt.

    d.   Soak equipment before washing.

What is the most serious case of an allergic reaction?

    a.   Vomiting

    b.   Migraine

    c.   Diarrhea

    d.   Anaphylactic shock

This occurs when allergens are transferred to a food that does not contain the allergen:

    a.   Cross Training

    b.   Cross Contamination

    c.   Cross Contact

    d.   Cross Control

Activity:

Complete your "The Big 9" poster and submit it for a vote with the class. The best posters can be displayed in the kitchen or classroom.

Section 3

Read the World Class Chicken Stock recipe carefully and list all known Time & Temperature Control for Safety (TCS) ingredients.

Video Assignment:

Watch the chicken stock video carefully and note any new skills needed.

Activity:

With your team, make a plan for what ingredients you can prepare for your mise en place. Make any needed alterations to the type of bones or vegetables for the type of stock being prepared.

In the Kitchen:

- Measure & weigh the raw ingredients for your team's chicken stock. Measure the needed cold water on the day you cook. Depending on your available class time, your team may need to roast the bones and cool them in preparation for tomorrow.
- Wrap and label all ingredients and store them appropriately.
- Create and record your equipment mise en place list with your team to prepare for tomorrow's lab.

Section 4

Prepare the chicken stock with your team. Read the grading rubric to achieve the maximum points available.

In the Kitchen:

Each team creates its mise en place for the chicken stock (preparation of ingredients & equipment needed).

The team will follow the recipe. Create the stock with any assistance needed from the instructor or the preparation video. The stock will be completed after the class has concluded (due to the simmering time required). Students will need to indicate times and write a plan for the teacher to chill the stock safely, using methods learned.

Each team should wash, rinse, and sanitize their equipment and work surfaces to the standards shown in the video and discussed in the coursebook.

Dirty		Clean
Hands		RTE Foods
Utensils		Utensils
Equipment		Equipment
Food contact surfaces		Food contact surfaces

Chicken stock chilling method chosen:

_____

_____

_____

_____

_____

_____

_____

_____

_____

_____

_____

_____

Section 5

Team presentation:

Each team will present a small amount of their stock, heated and lightly seasoned with salt & pepper. The teams will inspect each stock to see any flavor, clarity, and viscosity variances.

Activity:

The students should state their successes with their completed stock and what they would choose to do to make an improvement next time.

Recipe Cost Sheet:

Your instructor will assist you in filling out the recipe costing sheet.

Once completed, students should work out the recipe cost and then complete the per-portion price. With more practice, you will take the lead in completing costing sheets for projects you complete.

Watch and participate in the end-of-chapter review video.

Name:_____ Date: _____

Menu Item	
Number of Portions	Portion Size

Ingredient	Purchase Unit	Purchase cost	Unit cost	Amount Needed	Ingredient Cost

Total recipe cost	
Number of portions from recipe	
Portion Cost	

[Blank Page]

The "BIG 9" Grading Rubric

Students will see an example and professionally and accurately replicate the nine items for correctly identifying the most prominent allergens.

Students will be offered adequate time to complete this task, with scrutiny on their written information, safety and sanitation, accuracy, attractiveness and the quality of their finished product.

It is recommended that students use simple drawn examples to keep the information clear. Add some color to your work; a bold poster is eye appealing and will be more successful in educating others when on display.

Safety and accuracy are key to your success.

Culinary Arts
"The Big 9" Poster Rubric

Student name _____   Date _____

Category	Specifications	Highly Skilled (Professional) 25 pts	Skilled (First Cook) 20 pts	Moderately Skilled (Commis) 15pts	Low Skilled 10pts (Developing)	No Attempt 0pts	Comments
Written information 25pts	All written information is spelled correctly and is accurate	No guidance needed with all written information being accurate	Minimal guidance needed with all written information being accurate	Some guidance needed with all written information being accurate	Substantial guidance needed with all written information being accurate	No attempt made	
Safety & Sanitation 25pts	Correct information according to regulatory authority rules is presented	Exemplary standards maintained with no guidance	Very good standards maintained with some guidance	Good standards maintained, needed guidance	Poor standards maintained, needed guidance	No attempt made	
Accuracy of overall poster 25pts	Quality & precision of work, with accuracy of images and overall poster	Excellent precision with no guidance	Very good precision with some guidance	Good precision with guidance needed	Poor precision with guidance needed	No attempt made	
Quality of finished product 25pts	Final appearance of prepared poster with quality work achieved	Excellent quality finished poster, well presented	Very good quality finished poster, well presented	Good quality finished poster	Poor quality finished products	No attempt made	

Chicken Stock Rubric

Students will see the video example, safely, professionally and accurately replicating the chicken stock.

Students will be offered adequate time to complete this task, with scrutiny on their safety and sanitation, accuracy, attractiveness and the quality of their finished product.

Students should ensure all equipment and work surfaces are cleaned, sanitized and stored.

Safety and accuracy are key to your success.

Culinary Arts
Chicken Stock Recipe Rubric

Student name _____   Date _____

Category	Specifications	Highly Skilled (Professional) 25 pts	Skilled (First Cook) 20 pts	Moderately Skilled (Commis) 15pts	Low Skilled 10pts (Developing)	No Attempt 0pts	Comments
Accuracy reading & following the recipe (25pts Max)	Reading, comprehending & following the recipe is done with accuracy	No guidance needed with reading, comprehending & following the recipe.	Minimal guidance needed with reading, comprehending & following the recipe.	Some guidance needed with reading, comprehending & following the recipe	Substantial guidance needed with reading, comprehending & following the recipe	No attempt made	
Safety & Sanitation (25pts Max)	Correctly following all regulatory authority rules when preparing foods.	Exemplary standards maintained with no guidance	Very good standards maintained with some guidance	Good standards maintained, needed guidance	Poor standards maintained, needed guidance	No attempt made	
Accuracy & precision of preparations (25pts Max)	Accuracy & precision of work, with knife cuts & preparations.	Excellent precision with no guidance	Very good precision with some guidance	Good precision with guidance needed	Poor precision with guidance needed	No attempt made	
Quality of finished product (25pts Max)	Final appearance of prepared chicken stock with quality work achieved.	Excellent quality finished stock, well presented.	Very good quality finished stock, well presented.	Good quality finished stock.	Poor quality finished product.	No attempt made	

Chapter Summary

The theme of this chapter is to identify hazards and understand the necessary tools to prevent them from contaminating food. Managers must train and monitor staff on the steps necessary to avoid cross-contact, cross-contamination, and intentional contamination.

Preventing cross-contamination includes proper handwashing, protective coverings, good personal hygiene, separating raw ingredients from RTE foods, cleaning and sanitizing equipment, and using color-coded cutting boards. Avoiding cross-contact involves understanding that the Big 9 ingredients cannot come into contact with other foods to prevent serious allergic reactions. Finally, staff are the FIRST line of defense when it comes to preventing intentional contamination of food, with the goal of causing harm to others.

- Food contaminants include biological, physical, chemical, and allergens
- Cross-contamination happens when pathogens have been transferred to food
- Cross-contact happens when allergens are transferred to another food normally safe from allergens, creating a potential for an allergic reaction when consumed
- Intentional contamination, or adulterated food, happens when an individual deliberately contaminates food with the intention of harming others
- A food defense program is intended to combat intentional contamination
- A food safety program is intended to prevent accidental food contamination

Biological Hazards (Bad Bugs) *see chapter 3*
Bacteria, Viruses, Parasites, Yeast, Molds

Physical Hazards
Glass, Toothpicks, Fingernails, Jewelry

Chemical Hazards
Cleaners, Polishes, Sanitizers, Pesticides, Medications, First aid products, Metallic (elements/compounds)

Naturally Occurring Chemical Hazards
Fish toxins, Plant toxins

Allergen Hazards
The Big 9

The FDA created a program that managers can use to inform and remind food employees that they are the FIRST line of defense at preventing intentional food contamination.

ALERT

Assure
- Know your supplier
- Supervise offloading of incoming materials
- Request locked and/or sealed vehicles/containers/railcars

Look
- Implement a system for handling products
- Track materials
- Store product labels in a secure location and destroy outdated or discarded product labels
- Limit access and inspect facilities
- Keep track of finished products
- Encourage your warehousing operations to practice food defense measures

Employees
- Conduct background checks on staff
- Know who belongs in your facility
- Establish an identification system for employees
- Limit access by staff
- Prevent customer's access to critical areas of your facility

Reports
- Periodically evaluate the effectiveness of your security management system
- Perform random food defense inspections
- Establishment and maintenance of records
- Evaluate lessons learned

Threats
- Hold any product that you believe may have been affected
- Contact the Food and Drug Administration or USDA/Food Safety and Inspection Service

Chapter 5W

TCS Foods and Controls

The theme of this chapter is to understand the necessary controls to prevent foodborne illness, especially with Time/Temperature Control for Safety Foods (TCS Foods). Food managers must train to identify TCS Foods and properly monitor time and temperature.

This chapter covers the primary types of food hazards and the various controls used to prevent them from contaminating food. This involves understanding TCS foods, cross-contamination, intentional contamination, and the controls used to avoid foodborne illness. Controls are managerial methods used to implement, train, enforce, correct, retrain, and monitor food to ensure its safety within the flow of food. For example, thermometers are used to check a food's internal temperature, time is tracked to limit bacterial growth, and logs are kept to validate the process. All this and more are covered in this chapter.

Key Terms

Keep an eye out for these essential topics:

- Flow of Food
- Temperature danger zone
- Bimetallic Stemmed Thermometer
- Infrared Thermometer
- TCS foods
- Temperature measuring device
- Thermometer calibration
- Logs

Objectives

After working through this chapter, you should be able to explain the following to friends and family:

- Describe the flow of food
- Explain what TCS Foods are
- Describe the temperature danger zone
- Understand the types of thermometers and their uses
- Know how to calibrate a bimetallic thermometer
- Explain how to monitor time and temperature

Recipe

Recipe: Seafood Gumbo

Seafood gumbo is now popular across the U.S. and around the world. It is thought to have first originated in West Africa. The gelatinous nature of the okra added to the recipe would often be used to thicken the gumbo. The African word Ki Ngombo is okra. Today with so many generations, fusions, and available ingredients, we now enjoy many different tastes in our gumbos. But we owe its genesis to the culinary expertise from over 5000 miles away, on the African continent.

Ingredients:

- 1.5 cup vegetable oil
- 2 cups all-purpose flour
- 3 cups finely chopped onions
- 1.5 cup finely chopped green bell peppers
- 1.5 cup finely chopped celery
- 4 tablespoons minced garlic
- 1 gal fish stock (you can use a light chicken stock too)
- 1/2 teaspoon dried thyme
- 4 bay leaves
- 4 teaspoons Worcestershire sauce
- 3 teaspoons salt
- 1 teaspoon cayenne pepper
- 2 pound medium shrimp, peeled and deveined
- 2 pound white fish fillets, such as catfish, grouper, snapper, or tilapia
- 1/4 cup chopped fresh parsley
- 1/2 cup chopped tender green onion tops

Section 1

Reading assignment:

Read pages 87-98 in the coursebook, and then complete the activities below.

Fill in the missing words:

_____ _____ **Preparation**

There are always two or more complete trips through the temperature danger zone. This complex food preparation process usually involves foods prepared in large volumes or in advance for next-day service.

_____ **Preparation** _____

There is only one trip through the temperature danger zone. Food is usually cooked and held hot until served, e.g., fried chicken, but can also be cooked and served immediately.

_____ **Preparation** _____

There is no cook step to destroy pathogens. This category includes raw, ready-to-eat food like sashimi, raw oysters, and salads. Components of these foods are received raw and not cooked before consumption.

Questions:

In food safety, what are we referring to when we mention "The flow of foods"?

   a)   If the sauces have the correct consistency.
   b)   The path that food travels from receiving through service to the consumer.
   c)   If the food that was ordered from the server is correctly created in the kitchen.
   d)   The dishwasher pressure and temperatures are correctly set to clean the dishes & equipment.

When food passes through the temperature danger zone, it is at most risk in what range?

   a.   41-70 Fahrenheit (5-21 Celsius)
   b.   50-80 Fahrenheit (10-27 Celsius)
   c.   65-135 Fahrenheit (18-57 Celsius)
   d.   70-125 Fahrenheit (21-52 Celsius)

Which of the following are TCS foods?

   a.   Unwashed carrots
   b.   Sliced tomatoes
   c.   Raw potatoes
   d.   Uncut cantaloupe melon

Which type of thermometer is best suited to measure the surface of foods upon their arrival to the kitchen?

   a.   Bimetallic stemmed thermometer
   b.   Infrared thermometer
   c.   Candy/deep fryer thermometer
   d.   All of the above

Activity

Students will test the class bimetallic stemmed thermometers and recalibrate them if they are proven inaccurate with the instructor's assistance. Students will use the ice bath method, as it is the safest way to do this.

First, fill a two-cup or larger container with ice and cold water. DO NOT add anything else like salt. After a short time, insert the thermometer into the ice water, to the recording dimple, to gain an accurate measurement. Do not hold the thermometer by the stem, as the heat from the fingers can give an inaccurate reading. If the thermometer reaches 32 Fahrenheit (0 Celsius) the thermometer can be sanitized and put in a safe storage place. If not, students will recalibrate the thermometer using a small wrench on the calibration nut, located at the back of the thermometer face. Temperature accuracy is essential in food receiving, storage, cooking, holding and service.

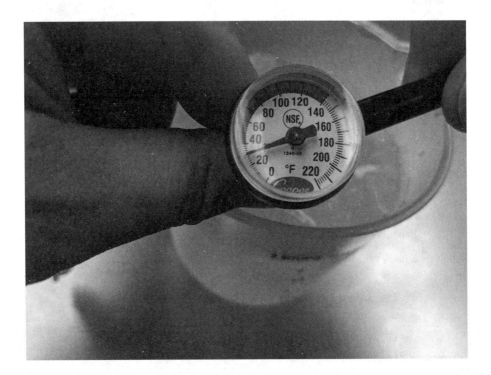

Section 2

Reading Assignment:

Read pages 98-103 in the coursebook, and then complete the activities below.

Fill in the missing words:

In addition to knowing _____ to calibrate a thermometer and measure a food's internal temperature, a food employee must also know _____ to take a measurement.

Questions:

What is RTE, with regards to food safety?

 a. Return To Eat
 b. Ready To Eat
 c. Ready To Enter
 d. Raise Temperature Edibility

When receiving foods, when should temperatures be taken?

 a. Within 2 hours
 b. Within 4 hours
 c. Within 6 hours
 d. Immediately

Refrigerated foods must be maintained at what internal temperature?

 a. 0 Fahrenheit (-18 Celsius)
 b. 32 Fahrenheit (0 Celsius)
 c. 41 Fahrenheit (5 Celsius)
 d. 45 Fahrenheit (7 Celsius)

When cooling foods, the first stage is to bring it to 70 Fahrenheit (21 Celsius). What is the maximum time allowed for this to occur?

 a. 30 minutes
 b. 2 hour
 c. 4 hours
 d. 6 hours

Activity:

Video Assignment:

Watch the seafood gumbo video carefully and note any new skills needed.

Section 3

Read the seafood gumbo recipe carefully and list all known Time & Temperature Control for Safety (TCS) and "BIG 9 allergen" ingredients.

Activity:

Today we will make the roux (the thickening agent) for the gumbo. This dark brown roux takes a long time to cook out and needs to be done with care, to avoid it burning, but encouraging the caramelization of the flour to enhance the flavors. At the same time one member of the cooking team is caring for the roux, the other members can be measuring the rest of the mise en place for the main cook tomorrow.

In the Kitchen:

- Add the oil and flour together and cook on medium heat, until the roux reaches the dark brown stage. Safely cool and refrigerate overnight.
- Measure and prepare all other ingredients needed for the recipe.
- Make a note of all the equipment that will be needed to fulfill the recipe tomorrow.

Section 4

Prepare the seafood gumbo with your team. Read the grading rubric to achieve the maximum points available.

In the Kitchen:

First heat the roux in a thick bottomed saucepan, suitable for cooking the gumbo. Use a medium heat, until it fully melts down. Follow all steps in the recipe to successfully create the seafood gumbo. Once completed, serve to customers you may have. With at least one portion, cool safely with the knowledge you have learned.

Wash, rinse & sanitize all equipment and tables used, completing this as a team.

Section 5

Activity:

Each team should heat a portion of their gumbo and examine any differences between them. Taste the different gumbos and take note of how variances in cooking can influence the outcome.

Note below what you would do differently next time to change or enhance the recipe:

_____

_____

_____

Discuss and note below ways to make the gumbo without the "Big 9" allergen items using alternate ingredients:

_____

_____

_____

Watch and participate in the end-of-chapter review video.

_____

_____

_____

_____

_____

_____

_____

_____

_____

_____

_____

_____

_____

_____

_____

_____

_____

Grading Rubric – Calibrate a bimetallic stemmed thermometer

Students will see an example and professionally and accurately understand how to calibrate a bimetallic stemmed thermometer.

Students will be offered adequate time to complete this task, with scrutiny on their reading information, safety and sanitation, accuracy and the quality of their finished calibrated thermometer.

Safety and accuracy are key to your success.

Culinary Arts

Calibrate Bimetallic Thermometer Rubric

Student name _____   Date _____

Category	Specifications	Highly Skilled (Professional) 25 pts	Skilled (First Cook) 20 pts	Moderately Skilled (Commis) 15pts	Low Skilled 10pts (Developing)	No Attempt 0pts	Comments
Reading information 25pts	All reading information is understood correctly and is accurate	No guidance needed with all reading information being accurate	Minimal guidance needed with all reading information being accurate	Some guidance needed with all reading information being accurate	Substantial guidance needed with all reading information being accurate	No attempt made	
Safety & Sanitation 25pts	Correct information according to regulatory authority rules is presented	Exemplary standards maintained with no guidance	Very good standards maintained with some guidance	Good standards maintained, needed guidance	Poor standards maintained, needed guidance	No attempt made	
Accuracy of calibration 25pts	Quality & precision of work, with accuracy of calibration	Excellent precision with no guidance	Very good precision with some guidance	Good precision with guidance needed	Poor precision with guidance needed	No attempt made	
Quality of finished product 25pts	Final appearance of calibrated quality work achieved	Excellent accuracy of finished thermometer presented	Very good accuracy of finished thermometer presented	Good accuracy of finished thermometer presented	Poor accuracy of finished thermometer presented	No attempt made	

Grading Rubric – Seafood gumbo recipe

Students will see the video example, safely, professionally and accurately replicating the seafood gumbo.

Students will be offered adequate time to complete this task, with scrutiny on their safety and sanitation, accuracy, attractiveness and the quality of their finished product.

Students should ensure all equipment and work surfaces are cleaned, sanitized and stored.

Safety and accuracy are key to your success.

Culinary Arts
Seafood Gumbo Recipe Rubric

Student name _____   Date _____

Category	Specifications	Highly Skilled (Professional) 25 pts	Skilled (First Cook) 20 pts	Moderately Skilled (Commis) 15pts	Low Skilled 10pts (Developing)	No Attempt 0pts	Comments
Accuracy reading & following the recipe (25pts Max)	Reading, comprehending & following the recipe is done with accuracy	No guidance needed, with reading, comprehending & following the recipe.	Minimal guidance needed with reading, comprehending & following the recipe.	Some guidance needed with reading, comprehending & following the recipe	Substantial guidance needed with reading, comprehending & following the recipe	No attempt made	
Safety & Sanitation (25pts Max)	Correctly following all regulatory authority rules when preparing foods.	Exemplary standards maintained with no guidance	Very good standards maintained with some guidance	Good standards maintained, needed guidance	Poor standards maintained, needed guidance	No attempt made	
Accuracy & precision of preparations (25pts Max)	Accuracy & precision of work, with knife cuts & preparations.	Excellent precision with no guidance	Very good precision with some guidance	Good precision with guidance needed	Poor precision with guidance needed	No attempt made	
Quality of finished product (25pts Max)	Final appearance of prepared seafood gumbo with quality work achieved.	Excellent quality finished gumbo, well presented.	Very good quality finished gumbo, well presented.	Good quality finished gumbo.	Poor quality finished product.	No attempt made	

Chapter Summary

The theme of this chapter is to understand the necessary controls to prevent foodborne illness, especially with Time/Temperature Control for Safety Foods (TCS Foods). Food managers must train to identify TCS Foods and properly monitor time and temperature.

When working with TCS Foods it is imperative they are not time and/or temperature abused. This requires the correct type of temperature measuring device that is properly calibrated. Food employees must also understand the temperature danger zone relative to the flow of food. For example, cooked food intended to be stored for later use must be cooled quickly from its final temperature, so the food spends minimal time in the temperature danger zone. The same is true when reheating the food for service. Finally, the necessary time and temperature measurements must be logged to ensure proper food safety controls are being followed.

- The FDA Food Code describes three primary preparation processes within the flow of food: No cook, same-day service, and complex preparation.
- TCS stands for: **T**ime/**T**emperature **C**ontrol for **S**afety.
- Foods that are susceptible to bacteria growth when in the temperature danger zone are considered TCS Foods.
- Color-coded cutting boards help keep raw ingredients separate from TCS foods.
- There are three primary types of thermometers: bimetallic, thermocouple/thermistor, and infrared.
- Bimetallic thermometers should be calibrated often using one of two methods: ice-point or boiling-point.
- Active managerial control means the manager, or person-in-charge (PIC), has implemented controls such as training and monitoring such that the food operation is fully compliant with the requirements of the Food Code.

Time/Temperature   **Control**   **Safety**

The **temperature danger zone** occurs when food is between 41°F–135°F (5°C–57°C). Within this range, bacterial growth potential is highest between 70°F–125°F (21°C–52°C).

Time/Temperature
Time and Temperature are monitored

Control
Proactive and reactive measures are taken to control time and temperature abuse

Safety
The goal is to prevent bacterial growth and keep food safe

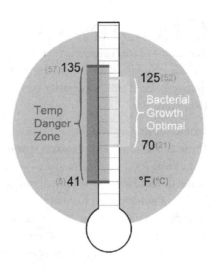

KEY TERM Time/Temperature Control for Safety Food (TCS Food) **is a food that requires time and/or temperature control for safety (TCS) to limit pathogenic growth or toxin formation.**

Foods prepared at the food operation may also become TCS Foods when they contain TCS Food ingredients. For example, a pie with meringue topping, meat salads, or fettuccine alfredo with chicken.

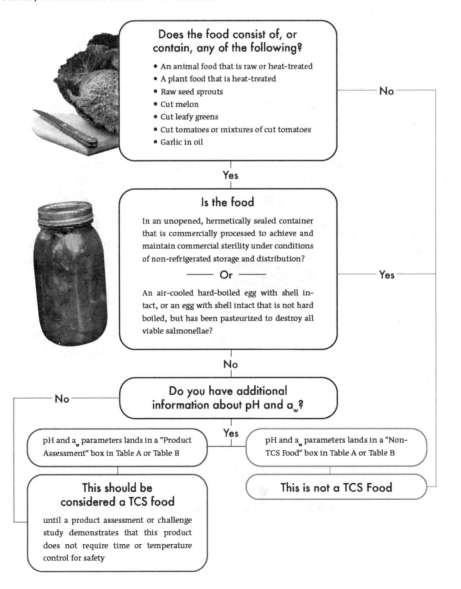

Does the food consist of, or contain, any of the following?

- An animal food that is raw or heat-treated
- A plant food that is heat-treated
- Raw seed sprouts
- Cut melon
- Cut leafy greens
- Cut tomatoes or mixtures of cut tomatoes
- Garlic in oil

No →

Yes ↓

Is the food

In an unopened, hermetically sealed container that is commercially processed to achieve and maintain commercial sterility under conditions of non-refrigerated storage and distribution?

—— Or ——

An air-cooled hard-boiled egg with shell intact, or an egg with shell intact that is not hard boiled, but has been pasteurized to destroy all viable salmonellae?

Yes →

No ↓

Do you have additional information about pH and a_w?

← No

Yes ↓

pH and a_w parameters lands in a "Product Assessment" box in Table A or Table B

pH and a_w parameters lands in a "Non-TCS Food" box in Table A or Table B

This should be considered a TCS food

until a product assessment or challenge study demonstrates that this product does not require time or temperature control for safety

This is not a TCS Food

Chapter 6W

Sources and Receiving

A manager has a lot of choices when it comes to the **source** of foods purchased for use in a food operation. Associated with those choices is a responsibility to follow the law and protect the consumer from contamination and food fraud. The U.S. government does its part to protect the source of foods by inspecting and grading them at the source to ensure they are pure, wholesome, and safe to eat. Food must be purchased from legal, approved, and reputable suppliers.

When **receiving** food during a delivery, trained staff supervised by management have a significant opportunity to safeguard the restaurant from a foodborne illness outbreak and financial loss. Some foods are not allowed to be used if they are not pasteurized, are not of the correct grade, are mislabeled, or missing the proper identification tags. Food can become contaminated at the processing plant or in transit through mishandling or temperature abuse and should therefore be rejected. Poor receiving practices can lead to financial hardships when food that could have easily been rejected at receiving can no longer be returned for a refund/replacement. Financial repercussions often occur due to a foodborne illness outbreak and the associated bad press, leading to business loss.

Key Terms

Keep an eye out for these essential topics:

- Wholesome
- Approved suppliers
- USDA Inspection stamp
- Grading
- Use-by dates
- Expiration dates
- Recalls
- Shellstock identification tag
- Key drop delivery

Objectives

After working through this chapter, you should be able to explain the following to friends and family:

- Describe the difference between U.S. Food Law and the FDA Food Code
- Explain USDA inspection and grading
- Appreciate the importance of good receiving practices
- Learn how to measure food temperature at receiving
- Explore the difference between acceptable foods and non-acceptable foods
- Understand the required receiving temperatures

Recipe .

Recipe: Broccoli & Cheddar Soup

Soups are categorized into two main choices: thick and clear. Clear soups are generally made with a stock as the base, like consommé or chicken noodle. The soup you will make is an example of a thick soup.

Ingredients:

- 4 tablespoons oil
- 1 medium yellow onion, diced
- 1 large carrot, diced
- 1 clove minced garlic
- 1/4 cup all-purpose flour
- 1 cup milk
- 5 cups chicken stock
- 6 cups broccoli (about 1 large head)
- 1/4 teaspoon nutmeg
- salt & pepper
- 8 ounces cheddar, shredded (about 2 cups)

Section 1

Reading assignment:

Read pages 107-115 in the coursebook, and then complete the activities below.

Fill in the missing words:

According to the FDA, the law intends to assure the consumer that foods are pure, _____, safe to eat, and produced under _____ conditions and that all labeling and packaging is _____, informative, and not deceptive.

Questions:

What authority forms the law that food handlers must abide by?

- a) State, local & tribal authorities
- b) FDA
- c) USDA
- d) FBI

What is the minimum grade acceptable to purchase milk for a restaurant kitchen?

- a. Grade A
- b. Grade A/B
- c. Grade B
- d. All of the above

When sourcing wild game meat, where must it be sourced?

- a. Hunters, if fabricated in a reputable facility, with refrigeration
- b. Commercially raised for food on a farm
- c. Hunters, if it is brought to the restaurant within 2 hours of the kill
- d. All of the above

What is Key Drop Delivery?

- a. A method restaurants use to deliver their food to repeat customers
- b. Busy restaurants drop a key in a box for delivery people to let themselves in the back door during lunch hours
- c. Restaurants who allow a delivery to be made outside of restaurant hours, with no immediate inspection of the delivery
- d. A smartphone app, which alerts the customer when the delivery driver passes into a 1km radius of their home for food delivery

Activity

Students will create a receiving poster, showing the appropriate temperatures for the stated categories of foods. This will assist the purchaser to make the decision to accept or reject foods entering the kitchen. Keep designs simple. Adding a little color can help to make it visually pleasing. The one with the highest vote (that is factually accurate) will be displayed in the kitchen, to be used as a guide. See the example below.

Receiving Criteria

**Cold TCS Foods
(Time & Temperature Controlled for Safety)
41 Fahrenheit or lower,** unless otherwise stated

Milk
**Receive at 45 Fahrenheit
Cool to 41 or below within
4 hours**

Eggs
**Receive at 45 Fahrenheit
Cool to 41 or below within
4 hours**

Live Shellstock (Mussels, scallops)
**Receive air temp 45 Fahrenheit
Internal temp 50 or lower
Cool to 41 or below within
4 hours**

Shucked Shellfish
**Receive at 45 Fahrenheit
Cool to 41 or below within
4 hours**

Frozen Food
**Receive at 0 Fahrenheit
or below. (Frozen solid)**

Hot TCS Foods
**Receive at 135
Fahrenheit
or higher**

Section 2

Reading Assignment:

Read pages 116-125 in the coursebook, and then complete the activities below.

Fill in the missing words:

Products should be received with _____ labels which comply with the law. Proper labels will, for example, indicate if products have _____, been pasteurized, or contain _____. Products missing labels should be rejected as part of a food defense program to limit possible intentional contamination.

Questions:

Which of the following are reasons to reject shell eggs?

    a. Broken shell or crack, but membrane intact and not leaking
    b. Adhering dirt, foreign material, or prominent stains
    c. Raw eggs not delivered in refrigerated equipment
    d. All of the above

Shellstock identification tags must be filed and kept by the restaurant for how many days after the last shellfish is sold or disposed of?

    a. 30
    b. 60
    c. 90
    d. 180

When receiving fin fish, what of the following characteristics should be present?

    a. Light ammonia aroma
    b. Soft flesh that yields when pressed
    c. Sitting in a pool of iced water
    d. Clear not sunken eyes

When receiving meat which of the following should NOT be present?

    a. No significant odor
    b. A slight slimy texture
    c. Firm texture
    d. Appropriate color

Activity:

Complete the receiving poster, ensuring accuracy and attractiveness. Keep the design simple, making it easy to read and use in your kitchen. Once all are completed the class should vote on their favorite to display in the receiving area.

Section 3

Read the broccoli & cheddar soup recipe carefully and list all known Time & Temperature Control for Safety (TCS) ingredients.

Video Assignment:

Watch the broccoli & cheddar soup video carefully and note any new skills needed.

Activity:

With your team, make a plan for what ingredients you can prepare for your mise en place. Make any needed alterations due to season or availability of products.

In the Kitchen:

- Measure & weigh the raw ingredients for your team's soup. Depending on available time, you may chop some of your vegetables today.
- Wrap and label all ingredients and store them appropriately.
- Create and record your equipment mise en place list with your team to be ready for tomorrow's practical.

Section 4

Prepare the soup with your team. Read the grading rubric to achieve the maximum points available.

In the Kitchen:
Each team creates their mise en place for the soup (preparation of ingredients & equipment needed).

The team will follow the recipe. Create the soup with any assistance needed from the instructor or the preparation video. Follow all steps in the recipe to successfully create the soup. Once completed, serve to customers you may have. With at least one portion, cool safely with the knowledge you have learned.

Wash, rinse & sanitize all equipment and tables used, completing this as a team.

Section 5

Team Presentation:

Each team should heat a portion of their soup and examine any differences between them. Taste the different soups and take note how variances in cooking can influence the outcome.

Note below what you would do differently next time to change or enhance the recipe:

_____
_____
_____
_____

Watch and participate in the end-of-chapter review video.

Activity:

Recipe Cost Sheet: Students can now work out the recipe cost sheet and then discover the per-portion price.

_____
_____
_____
_____
_____
_____
_____
_____
_____
_____
_____
_____
_____
_____
_____
_____
_____
_____
_____

Recipe Cost Worksheet

Name:_____ Date: _____

Menu Item	
Number of Portions		Portion Size	

Ingredient	Purchase Unit	Purchase cost	Unit cost	Amount Needed	Ingredient Cost

Total recipe cost	
Number of portions from recipe	
Portion Cost	

[Blank Page]

Grading Rubric- Receiving Poster

Students will see an example and professionally and accurately replicate a poster depicting the rules of receiving foods safely.

Students will be offered adequate time to complete this task, with scrutiny on their written information, safety and sanitation, accuracy, attractiveness and the quality of their finished product.

It is recommended that students use simple drawn examples to keep the information clear. Add some color to your work, as a bold poster is eye appealing and will be more successful in educating others when on display.

Safety and accuracy are key to your success.

Culinary Arts
Receiving Poster Rubric

Student name _____   Date _____

Category	Specifications	Highly Skilled (Professional) 25 pts	Skilled (First Cook) 20 pts	Moderately Skilled (Commis) 15pts	Low Skilled 10pts (Developing)	No Attempt 0pts	Comments
Written information 25pts	All written information is spelled correctly and is accurate	No guidance needed with all written information being accurate	Minimal guidance needed with all written information being accurate	Some guidance needed with all written information being accurate	Substantial guidance needed with all written information being accurate	No attempt made	
Safety & Sanitation 25pts	Correct information according to regulatory authority rules is presented	Exemplary standards maintained with no guidance	Very good standards maintained with some guidance	Good standards maintained, needed guidance	Poor standards maintained, needed guidance	No attempt made	
Accuracy of overall poster 25pts	Quality & precision of work, with accuracy of images and overall poster	Excellent precision with no guidance	Very good precision with some guidance	Good precision with guidance needed	Poor precision with guidance needed	No attempt made	
Quality of finished product 25pts	Final appearance of prepared poster with quality work achieved	Excellent quality finished poster, well presented	Very good quality finished poster, well presented	Good quality finished poster	Poor quality finished products	No attempt made	

Grading Rubric- Broccoli & Cheddar Soup

Students will see the video example, safely, professionally and accurately replicating the broccoli & cheddar soup.

Students will be offered adequate time to complete this task, with scrutiny on their safety and sanitation, accuracy, attractiveness and the quality of their finished product.

Students should ensure all equipment and work surfaces are cleaned, sanitized and stored.

Safety and accuracy are key to your success.

Culinary Arts

Broccoli Cheddar Soup Recipe Rubric

Student name _____   Date _____

Category	Specifications	Highly Skilled (Professional) 25 pts	Skilled (First Cook) 20 pts	Moderately Skilled (Commis) 15pts	Low Skilled 10pts (Developing)	No Attempt 0pts	Comments
Accuracy reading & following the recipe (25pts Max)	Reading, comprehending & following the recipe is done with accuracy	No guidance needed with reading, comprehending & following the recipe.	Minimal guidance needed with reading, comprehending & following the recipe.	Some guidance needed with reading, comprehending & following the recipe	Substantial guidance needed with reading, comprehending & following the recipe	No attempt made	
Safety & Sanitation (25pts Max)	Correctly following all regulatory authority rules when preparing foods.	Exemplary standards maintained with no guidance	Very good standards maintained with some guidance	Good standards maintained, needed guidance	Poor standards maintained, needed guidance	No attempt made	
Accuracy & precision of preparations (25pts Max)	Accuracy & precision of work, with knife cuts & preparations.	Excellent precision with no guidance	Very good precision with some guidance	Good precision with guidance needed	Poor precision with guidance needed	No attempt made	
Quality of finished product (25pts Max)	Final appearance of prepared Broccoli Cheddar soup with quality work achieved.	Excellent quality finished soup, well presented.	Very good quality finished soup, well presented.	Good quality finished soup.	Poor quality finished product.	No attempt made	

Chapter Summary

The theme of this chapter is to understand the source of foods and the proper receiving practices. Management often orders products to be delivered and is responsible for understanding the associated laws and best practices. Properly trained staff who take their time to inspect food during deliveries will be effective in preventing unwanted products from entering the facility. Suitable receiving methods include a sensory inspection, looking for discoloration, smelling for off odors, touching for texture, and measuring for required temperatures.

When receiving TCS Foods it is imperative they are not time and/or temperature abused. They should be delivered in a refrigerated truck and their temperatures checked. Signs of previous temperature abuse should also be assessed. Most TCS foods are to be delivered at 41°F (5°C) or below with some exceptions, like whole eggs may be received at 45°F (7°C) or below.

- The U.S. Food Law are federal laws passed by Congress.
- The FDA Food Code is not law until/unless adopted by a state, county, city, or tribal authority.
- Good receiving practices can prevent foodborne illness and financial loss.
- Use the appropriate method to measure the temperature of food at delivery:
    - Meat: probe inserted into the thickest part
    - ROP: probe placed between two packages, not penetrating the packaging
    - Packaged foods: remove lid and insert the probe
    - Fruits and vegetables: measure surface temp with infrared, not penetrating product
- Staff look for discoloration, smell for off odors, touch for texture, and measure for required temperatures.
- Molluscan shellfish, shellstock, and finfish must be received clean, without broken shells, alive (shellstock), and with proper labeling and/or identification tags.

Tags must be kept on file for 90 days to trace the shellstock back to its original source in case of a foodborne illness outbreak. This timeframe, as listed below, accounts for the incubation and discovery of the typical worst-case virus scenario, hepatitis A.

Why 90 days?

Shelf-life of the product	14 days
Incubation perios	56 days
Medical diagnosis and confirmation	5 days
Reporting	5 days
Epidemiological investigation	10 days
Total:	90 days

What are egg products?

The term "egg products" refers to eggs that are removed from their shells for processing, which includes breaking eggs, filtering, mixing, stabilizing, blending, pasteurizing, cooling, freezing, drying, and packaging. This is done at plants inspected by the United States Department of Agriculture (USDA).

The following foods must be received at the specified temperatures:

- Refrigerated TCS Foods: 41°F (5°C) or below
- Raw eggs: 45°F (7°C) or below
- Milk   45°F (7°C) or below   cool to 41
  < 4 hours
- Shucked shellfish   45°F (7°C)   cool to 41 < 4 hours
- Shellstock (Live shellfish)   45°F (7°C) (internal 50F) cool to 41 < 4hr
- Cooked TCS Foods received
  hot for service: 135°F (57°C) or above
- Foods labeled and shipped frozen   Frozen

From the FDA Food Code:

If food is being delivered during the inspection, inspectors should:

- Verify internal product temperatures

- Examine package integrity upon delivery

- Look for signs of temperature abuse (e.g., large ice crystals in the packages of frozen products)

- Examine delivery truck and products for potential for cross-contamination

- Observe the food establishment's behaviors and practices as they relate to the establishment's control of contamination and holding and cooling temperatures of received products

- Review receiving logs and other documents, product labels, and food products to ensure that foods are received from regulated food processing plants (no foods prepared at home) and at the proper temperature.

Inspectors should look to see that raw animal foods and ready-to-eat foods are separated during receiving, storage, and preparation.

Chapter 7W
Storage

Storage is usually the next stop for food once it has been received within a food operation. The big things to understand are proper containers, labeling, date marking, rotation, temperature, and contamination control.

Food operations have three primary types of food storage spaces: dry, refrigerated, and frozen. These spaces must be well maintained and monitored to ensure food is fresh, free of contaminants, and kept at the proper temperatures. Food that becomes expired, contaminated, or time/temperature abused in storage must be discarded. Failure to properly manage stored food often leads to foodborne illness.

Since food storage spaces are often out of sight, they may also be out of mind. Meaning that, since they are not used as often as other spaces, they could be overlooked. Therefore, a food manager must develop staff training, procedures, and logs to ensure storage spaces are in tip-top shape. Doing so will also help facilitate a smooth inspection by the health department.

Key Terms
Keep an eye out for these essential topics:

- Walk-in cooler
- Date marking
- First-in, First-out (FIFO) method
- Reduced Oxygen Packaging (ROP) Foods
- Reconditioned
- Comminuted
- Condensate
- Working containers

Objectives
After working through this chapter, you should be able to explain the following to friends and family:

- Describe the types of food storage spaces
- Understand the vertical food storage requirements
- Learn about the importance of date marking
- Describe the purpose of first-in, first-out (FIFO)
- Understand what cannot be placed in a food storage space
- Explain the temperature requirements for stored food

Recipe

Recipe: Steak & Baked Potato with Broccoli

Students will now put together a full entrée to present and enjoy. Selecting a steak is important. There are different grades and cuts that can affect the outcome. Some steaks are selected for flavor and are suitable for slow cooking (often from the front end of the steer) to tenderize them, like brisket. Other steaks from areas like the loin are tender and require faster, rapid but relatively short cooking methods, so they maintain their tender and moist texture. Cost can also be a defining factor in your choice of steak, as it is prized financially too.

Steak, as we know, needs to be cooked to 145 Fahrenheit internal temperature. However, unless you are cooking for someone in the high-risk populations, it is acceptable to cook the steak to a lower degree. Below are some degrees we cook steaks to the taste of the customer. Steaks are removed when they are approximately five degrees lower than the required temperature, as carryover cooking, which occurs when the steak rests, will raise the core temperature further. It is important to remember that all restaurants must have a warning for the customer on their menu that they are taking on the risk when they order and consume undercooked foods.

Rare	Medium-Rare	Medium	Medium-Well	Well Done
125°F (52°C)	135° (57°C)	145°F (63°C)	150°F (66°C)	160°F (71°C)

Ingredients:

- 2 x 6-8 oz. steak (NY strip is used in the video)
- 8 oz. butter
- rosemary (fresh or dried)
- vegetable oil
- 2 large baking potatoes
- 4 oz. sharp cheddar
- 6 oz. fresh broccoli
- sea salt & pepper

Section 1

Reading assignment:

Read pages 129-138 in the coursebook, and then complete the activities below.

Fill in the missing words:

Dry storage is meant explicitly for _____ items and _____ _____ that is not _____ control for safety (TCS) food. This includes canned goods, dried goods, tableware, carry-out utensils, straws, containers, placemats, stirrers, toothpicks, etc.

Questions:

What temperature must a refrigerator be?

a. 0 Fahrenheit (-18 Celsius) or below
b. 32 Fahrenheit (0 Celsius) or below
c. 41 Fahrenheit (5 Celsius) or below
d. 50 Fahrenheit (10 Celsius) or below

What temperature must a freezer be?

a. 0 Fahrenheit (-18 Celsius) or below
b. 32 Fahrenheit (0 Celsius) or below
c. 41 Fahrenheit (5 Celsius) or below
d. 50 Fahrenheit (10 Celsius) or below

What temperature must dry storage (ambient) be?

a. 0-32 Fahrenheit (-18 - 0 Celsius)
b. 32-41 Fahrenheit (0 – 5 Celsius)
c. 50-70 Fahrenheit (10-21 Celsius)
d. 60-80 Fahrenheit (16-27 Celsius)

What is the difference between the cooked minimum internal temperature of fish and steaks?

a. 0 Fahrenheit
b. 10 Fahrenheit
c. 15 Fahrenheit
d. 20 Fahrenheit

Activity

Students will create a poster showing the appropriate placement of foods in a refrigerator. The minimum core temperatures for the food items in that shelf will also be reflected. This will assist all students to make the best decision on where to store foods safely, minimizing the risk of cross contamination. Keep designs simple. Adding a little color can help to make it visually pleasing. The one with the highest vote (that is factually accurate) will be displayed in the kitchen, to be used as a guide. See the example below.

Section 2

Reading Assignment:

Read pages 139-151 in the coursebook, and then complete the activities below.

Fill in the missing words:

Ready-to-eat TCS foods are presumed to have safe levels of _____ when received and stored in a walk-in cooler. While TCS foods are properly refrigerated, bacterial growth is _____ but not completely stopped. Therefore, ready-to-eat TCS foods stored for extended periods can become _____ and unsafe for consumption.

Questions:

Once a ready-to-eat TCS food is prepared or a container opened, the storage container must be date marked if held for more than:

    a.   12 hours

    b.   24 hours

    c.   36 hours

    d.   7 days

Ready-to-eat TCS foods can be stored for a maximum of _ days when refrigerated at 41°F (5°C) or below.

    a.   1

    b.   5

    c.   7

    d.   14

The FDA Food Code recommends a product rotation method called FIFO. What does it stand for?

    a.   First In, Former Out

    b.   First Imaged, First Out

    c.   First In, First Out

    d.   Finite in, Fused Out

What shelf do we store raw poultry on, such as chicken and turkey?

    a.   Top shelf

    b.   Second shelf

    c.   Any shelf, if well wrapped

    d.   Bottom shelf

Activity:

Complete the refrigerator placement poster, ensuring accuracy and attractiveness. Keep the design simple, making it easy to read and use in your kitchen. Once all are completed the class should vote on their favorite to display on the refrigerator.

Section 3

Read the steak & baked potato recipe carefully and list all known Time & Temperature Control for Safety (TCS) ingredients.

Video Assignment:

Watch the steak & baked potato video carefully and note any new skills needed.

Activity:

With your team, make a plan for what ingredients you can prepare for your mise en place. Make any needed alterations due to season, price or availability of products.

In the Kitchen:

- Measure & weigh the raw ingredients for your team's meal. Depending on available time, you may chop the broccoli today.

- Wrap and label all ingredients and store them appropriately.

- Create and record your equipment mise en place list with your team to be ready for tomorrow's practical.

Section 4

Prepare the steak & baked potato with your team. Read the grading rubric, to achieve the maximum points available.

In the Kitchen:

Each team creates their mise en place for the meal (preparation of ingredients & equipment needed).

The team will follow the recipe. Create the meal with any assistance needed from the instructor or the preparation video. Follow all steps in the recipe to successfully create the dish. Your team should choose the temperatures you desire to cook your steaks. Choose two different temperatures. Once completed, record the presentation of your steak with a photograph and send to your instructor. Allow others in your class to taste your team's results. Take note of the difference in temperatures cooked, for tomorrow's exercise.

Wash, rinse & sanitize all equipment and tables used, completing this as a team.

Section 5

Team Presentation:

Each team should briefly report on their steak and baked potato dishes -- the temperatures and the differences noted between them. The class should also discuss the different presentations made by the teams.

Note below what you would do differently next time to change or enhance the recipe:

Watch and participate in the end-of-chapter review video.

Activity:

Recipe Cost Sheet: Students can now work out the recipe cost sheet and then discover the per-portion price.

Name:_____ Date: _____

Menu Item	
Number of Portions	Portion Size

Ingredient	Purchase Unit	Purchase cost	Unit cost	Amount Needed	Ingredient Cost

Total recipe cost	
Number of portions from recipe	
Portion Cost	

[Blank Page]

Grading Rubric - Refrigerator Guide

Students will see an example and professionally and accurately replicate the different levels in a commercial refrigerator, to safely store foods.

-Ready to Eat (RTE)　　　　　　　(Minimum internal cooking temp)

-Seafood　　　　　　　　　　　(145 Fahrenheit)

-Intact whole cuts of beef, pork, veal(145 Fahrenheit)

-Non-intact ground, mechanically　(155 Fahrenheit)

tenderized beef, pork, veal

-Whole & ground poultry　　　　　(165 Fahrenheit)

Students will be offered adequate time to complete this task, with scrutiny on their written information, safety and sanitation, accuracy, attractiveness, and the quality of their finished product.

It is recommended that students use simple drawn examples to keep the information clear. Add some color to your work, as a bold poster is eye appealing and will be more successful in educating others when on display.

Safety and accuracy are key to your success.

Culinary Arts
Refrigerator Poster Rubric

Student name _____   Date _____

Category	Specifications	Highly Skilled (Professional) 25 pts	Skilled (First Cook) 20 pts	Moderately Skilled (Commis) 15pts	Low Skilled 10pts (Developing)	No Attempt 0pts	Comments
Written information 25pts	All written information is spelled correctly and is accurate	No guidance needed with all written information being accurate	Minimal guidance needed with all written information being accurate	Some guidance needed with all written information being accurate	Substantial guidance needed with all written information being accurate	No attempt made	
Safety & Sanitation 25pts	Correct information according to regulatory authority rules are followed	Exemplary standards maintained with no guidance	Very good standards maintained with some guidance	Good standards maintained, needed guidance	Poor standards maintained, needed guidance	No attempt made	
Accuracy of overall poster 25pts	Quality & precision of work, with accuracy of images and overall poster	Excellent precision with no guidance	Very good precision with some guidance	Good precision with guidance needed	Poor precision with guidance needed	No attempt made	
Quality of finished product 25pts	Final appearance of prepared poster with quality work achieved	Excellent quality finished poster, well presented	Very good quality finished poster, well presented	Good quality finished poster	Poor quality finished products	No attempt made	

Grading Rubric - Steak & Baked Potato Recipe

Students will see the video example, safely, professionally, and accurately replicating the steak & potato recipe.

Students will be offered adequate time to complete this task, with scrutiny on their safety and sanitation, accuracy, attractiveness, and quality of their finished product.

Students should ensure all equipment and work surfaces are cleaned, sanitized and stored.

Safety and accuracy are key to your success.

Culinary Arts
Steak & Potato Recipe Rubric

Student name _____　　　　Date _____

Category	Specifications	Highly Skilled (Professional) 25 pts	Skilled (First Cook) 20 pts	Moderately Skilled (Commis) 15pts	Low Skilled 10pts (Developing)	No Attempt 0pts	Comments
Accuracy reading & following the recipe (25pts Max)	Reading, comprehending & following the recipe is done with accuracy	No guidance needed with reading, comprehending & following the recipe.	Minimal guidance needed with reading, comprehending & following the recipe.	Some guidance needed with reading, comprehending & following the recipe	Substantial guidance needed with reading, comprehending & following the recipe	No attempt made	
Safety & Sanitation (25pts Max)	Correctly following all regulatory authority rules when preparing foods.	Exemplary standards maintained with no guidance	Very good standards maintained with some guidance	Good standards maintained, needed guidance	Poor standards maintained, needed guidance	No attempt made	
Accuracy & precision of preparations (25pts Max)	Accuracy & precision of work, with knife cuts & preparations.	Excellent precision with no guidance	Very good precision with some guidance	Good precision with guidance needed	Poor precision with guidance needed	No attempt made	
Quality of finished product (25pts Max)	Final appearance of prepared Steak & Potato with quality work achieved.	Excellent quality finished meal, well presented.	Very good quality finished meal, well presented.	Good quality finished meal.	Poor quality finished product.	No attempt made	

Chapter Summary

The theme of this chapter is to understand how food is to be safely stored until needed within a food operation. This involves describing the types of storage and their associated temperatures. It also includes knowing what requires date marking and how to rotate food, so the older products are used first. When a food manager trains and monitors staff on these essential topics, the operation will minimize lost revenue due to wasted food and avoid disastrous foodborne illness outbreaks.

Remember these food storage basics:

- Store RTE foods separately from raw foods to prevent cross-contamination
- Separate fish, raw meat, and poultry
- Keep food in clean containers or wrappers
- Keep storage areas, dollies, and food-transporting carts clean and dry
- Never store trash or soiled equipment in a food storage space
- Keep all chemicals in their original labeled containers
- Store chemicals away from food
- Store food at least 6 inches off of the floor

Temperatures:

- Dry Storage   50°F – 70°F (10°C – 21°C)
- Refrigerated Storage   41°F (5°C) or below
- Frozen Storage   0°F (-18°C) or below

Vertical order, top to bottom	Min internal cook temperature
Washed, cut tomatoes	Not applicable
Ready-to-eat food, fully cooked food, fresh produce	Not applicable
Seafood, eggs	145°F (63°C)
Intact beef, pork, veal, lamb	145°F (63°C)
Non-intact comminuted: Ground meat, ground fish	155°F (68°C)
Poultry (Whole & ground)	165°F (73°C)

[Blank Page]

Chapter 8W
Food Preparation

Consuming cooked food is one of the main reasons people go out to eat. This chapter covers the important aspects of food preparation. As always, a recurring theme will be that of food safety and preventing foodborne illness, to keep the consumer safe and coming back for more!

The **preparation** process often begins with the need to thaw food. The process of thawing food is important and should never be done at room temperature (even at home) as too much time is spent in the temperature danger zone and bacteria can quickly multiply to unsafe levels.

The next step involves **cooking** the food to the proper minimum internal temperature, for a minimum amount of time, to inactivate pathogens. The combination of time and temperature varies based on the type of food and if it has been processed. There are also special restrictions related to serving raw or undercooked food when requested by a consumer.

If the cooked food is not meant for immediate service or is intentionally partially cooked, there are specific **post-cooking** requirements to keep the food safe for later consumption. This includes quickly cooling and then, later, quickly reheating the food to minimize the time spent in the temperature danger zone.

Key Terms
Keep an eye out for these essential topics:

- Additives
- Slacking
- Pooled eggs
- Variance
- Regulatory authority
- Minimum internal temperature
- Partial cooking
- Customer Advisories

Objectives
After working through this chapter, you should be able to explain the following to friends and family:

- Understand how to safely thaw TCS foods
- Learn about working with fresh produce
- Describe the minimum internal cooking temperatures
- Understand the importance of consumer advisories
- Describe the proper cooling requirements
- Explain the restrictions for highly susceptible populations

Recipe

Recipe: Tomato Sauce

Tomato sauce is one of our five mother sauces. This means this is a basic sauce in which we can add one or more extra ingredients to create a derivative sauce, which we will use in many different dishes. It is a building block, much like the chicken stock we produced in chapter 4. We will make this tomato sauce, chill, and freeze it, with the plan to use it with other components to make a meal later. In other words, we are making this sauce as part of our later mise en place.

Ingredients:

- 1/4 cup vegetable oil
- 1/2 medium onion, small dice
- 1 stick celery, small dice
- 1 carrot, small dice
- 1tsp ground garlic
- 28oz canned tomatoes (or fresh, if in season)
- 1 tsp dried basil

Section 1

Reading assignment:

Read pages 155-167 in the coursebook, and then complete the activities below.

Fill in the missing words:

Food preparation involves processing, seasoning, _____, and/or combining products and ingredients from _____ and _____ sources. The prepared food is available for immediate service or stored for later use.

Questions:

What is the best way to defrost TCS foods?

    a)   In the microwave.
    b)   In the refrigerator.
    c)   Under running cold water.
    d)   Wrapped on a counter in a cool room.

What is a good choice for defrosting burgers, straight out of the freezer?

    a.   Place them straight on the grill and defrost as part of the cooking process.
    b.   Run them under chilled running water.
    c.   In the microwave.
    d.   Leave them next to the grill to warm slowly.

What does the abbreviation ROP stand for?

    a.   Reliable Oxygenated Packaging.
    b.   Retained Oxygen Packaging.
    c.   Related Oxygen Packaging.
    d.   Reduced Oxygen Packaging.

In the three-step breading process, once the flour has been contaminated with the egg dip, it must be:

    a.   Eaten within six hours.
    b.   Treated as a TCS food and stored or disposed of accordingly.
    c.   Dried out, to stop bacterial growth.
    d.   Disposed of within 15 minutes of breading.

Activity

Each student will create a petri dish, using their phone (or outer case) as the subject of investigation. We shower, put on clean clothes every day, and tote around a filthy phone, which is rarely cleaned. Take a slice of fresh bread, one which is from a bakery and not a pre-sliced bread, as they have too many preservatives. Gently wipe one side of the bread on one side of the phone and turn them over and wipe the other face of the phone on the other side of the bread. Seal them into a zip sandwich bag. They should be placed in a container in a dark, room temperature space for the next two weeks.

Section 2

Reading Assignment:

Read pages 168-181 in the coursebook, and then complete the activities below.

Fill in the missing words:

Specific rules apply when fresh _____ is packaged in a food _____ as opposed to being sourced from a _____ processing facility.

Questions:

What is a variance?

    a.   It allows a food operation to do something otherwise not permitted by the regulatory authority or food code.

    b.   A change granted by the chef in a large banquet.

    c.   Changes written on the server ticket for a table in the restaurant.

    d.   The difference found in meat colors, for instance, a frozen or fresh beef steak.

Who are in the Highly Susceptible Populations?

    a.   Preschool children.

    b.   Compromised immune system.

    c.   Elderly adults.

    d.   All of the above.

What temperature must plant-based foods be cooked to?

    a.   135 Fahrenheit.

    b.   145 Fahrenheit.

    c.   155 Fahrenheit.

    d.   165 Fahrenheit.

When cooking in a microwave, what temperature must be achieved, with all foods?

    a.   135 Fahrenheit.

    b.   145 Fahrenheit.

    c.   155 Fahrenheit.

    d.   165 Fahrenheit.

Individual Activity:

Complete the exercise on the following page.

Name:_____ Date: _____

Is it safe?

Let's see how you would react to the following data, if you were a Food Safety Manager and had to keep your customers safe...

A 50-pound pot of chili came off the stove to cool at 3 pm. It hit 135 Fahrenheit (57 Celsius) at 3:30 pm. By 5 pm, it is now down to 89 Fahrenheit (31 Celsius). What would you do?

Nothing, it should be fine.	Get it on ice, to speed up cooling.	Get it in the refrigerator quickly.	Reheat and try to cool again.

	Safe	Unsafe	Need more info
Commercially produced fried cheese sticks 135°F (57°C)			
Hamburger to go in a bun with French fries 145°F (63°C)			
Tilapia, deep-fried and served with tartar sauce 145°F (63°C)			
Beef tenderloin, roasted 135°F (57°C)			
Broccoli cooked with melted butter and hot held on the buffet 130°F (54°C)			
Pork chop, grilled 145°F (63°C)			
Turkey, roasted for Thanksgiving 135°F (57°C)			
Grilled sweet peppers 135°F (57°C)			
Stuffed chicken breast, with asparagus 165°F (74°C)			
Shrimp stuffed salmon, grilled with asparagus 145°F (63°C)			

35 pounds of beef stew is cooling. It hit 135 Fahrenheit (57 Celsius) at 11:30 am. It is now at 1:30 pm, and it is at 69 Fahrenheit (21°C). What would you do?

Nothing, it should be fine.	Get it on ice, to speed up cooling.	Get it in the refrigerator quickly.	Stir it occasionally.

Now let's compare to the rest of the class, how you decided on what was acceptable or needed to be changed.

Section 3

Read the tomato sauce recipe carefully and list all known Time & Temperature Control for Safety (TCS) ingredients.

Video Assignment:

Watch the tomato sauce video carefully and note any new skills needed.

Activity:

With your team, make a plan for what ingredients you can prepare for your mise en place. Make any needed alterations due to season or availability of products, like fresh or canned tomatoes.

In the Kitchen:

- Measure & weigh the raw ingredients for your team's sauce. Depending on available time, you may chop the vegetables and blanch and skin the tomatoes, if using fresh, today.
- Wrap and label all ingredients and store them appropriately.
- Create and record your equipment mise en place list with your team to be ready for tomorrow's practical.

Section 4

Prepare the tomato sauce with your team. Read the grading rubric, to achieve the maximum points available.

In the Kitchen:

Each team creates its mise en place for the sauce (preparation of ingredients & equipment needed).

The team will follow the recipe. Create the sauce with any assistance needed from the instructor or the preparation video. Follow all steps in the recipe to successfully create the sauce. Make sure to lightly season the sauce, as you will add additional ingredients later.

Your team will need to rapidly cool the sauce to safe levels, 70 Fahrenheit (21°C) or lower, before placing it into the refrigerator.

Wash, rinse & sanitize all equipment and tables used, completing this as a team.

Activity:

Complete the cooling log for your sauce.

Name:_____ Date: _____

Cooling Temperature Log

Date	Initials	Food Product	Cooling Time/Temperature						Corrective Action
			Final Temp	Time	2 Hrs	Time	4 Hrs	Time	

[Blank Page]

Section 5

Team Presentation:

Each team should heat a portion of their sauce and examine any differences between them. Taste the different sauces and take note how variances in cooking can influence the outcome.

Note below what you would do differently next time to change or enhance the recipe:

Watch and participate in the end-of-chapter review video.

Activity:

Recipe Cost Sheet:

Students can now work out the recipe cost sheet and then discover the per-portion price.

Recipe Cost Worksheet

Name:_____ Date: _____

Menu Item	
Number of Portions		Portion Size	

Ingredient	Purchase Unit	Purchase cost	Unit cost	Amount Needed	Ingredient Cost

Total recipe cost	
Number of portions from recipe	
Portion Cost	

[Blank Page]

Grading Rubric- Is It Safe Game?

Students will use their knowledge built up so far and do their best to adapt that to these real-life situations.

Students will be offered adequate time to complete this task, with scrutiny of their written information, safety and sanitation, accuracy, attractiveness, and the quality of their finished document.

Safety and accuracy are key to your success.

Culinary Arts
Is It Safe? Rubric

Student name _____   Date _____

Category	Specifications	Highly Skilled (Professional) 25 pts	Skilled (First Cook) 20 pts	Moderately Skilled (Commis) 15pts	Low Skilled 10pts (Developing)	No Attempt 0pts	Comments
Written information 25pts	All written information is spelled correctly and is accurate	No guidance needed with all written information being accurate	Minimal guidance needed with all written information being accurate	Some guidance needed with all written information being accurate	Substantial guidance needed with all written information being accurate	No attempt made	
Safety & Sanitation 25pts	Correct information according to regulatory authority rules is presented	Exemplary standards maintained with no guidance	Very good standards maintained with some guidance	Good standards maintained, needed guidance	Poor standards maintained, needed guidance	No attempt made	
Accuracy of overall document 25pts	Quality & precision of work, with accuracy of information	Excellent precision with no guidance	Very good precision with some guidance	Good precision with guidance needed	Poor precision with guidance needed	No attempt made	
Quality of finished document 25pts	Final appearance of prepared document with quality work achieved	Excellent quality finished document, well presented	Very good quality finished document, well presented	Good quality finished document	Poor quality finished products	No attempt made	

Grading Rubric- Tomato Sauce

Students will see the video example, safely, professionally and accurately replicating the tomato sauce.

Students will be offered adequate time to complete this task, with scrutiny on their safety and sanitation, accuracy, attractiveness and the quality of their finished product.

Students should ensure all equipment and work surfaces are cleaned, sanitized and stored.

Safety and accuracy are key to your success.

Culinary Arts
Tomato Sauce Recipe Rubric

Student name _____   Date _____

Category	Specifications	Highly Skilled (Professional) 25 pts	Skilled (First Cook) 20 pts	Moderately Skilled (Commis) 15pts	Low Skilled 10pts (Developing)	No Attempt 0pts	Comments
Accuracy reading & following the recipe (25pts Max)	Reading, comprehending & following the recipe is done with accuracy	No guidance needed with reading, comprehending & following the recipe.	Minimal guidance needed with reading, comprehending & following the recipe.	Some guidance needed with reading, comprehending & following the recipe	Substantial guidance needed with reading, comprehending & following the recipe	No attempt made	
Safety & Sanitation (25pts Max)	Correctly following all regulatory authority rules when preparing foods.	Exemplary standards maintained with no guidance	Very good standards maintained with some guidance	Good standards maintained, needed guidance	Poor standards maintained, needed guidance	No attempt made	
Accuracy & precision of preparations (25pts Max)	Accuracy & precision of work, with knife cuts & preparations.	Excellent precision with no guidance	Very good precision with some guidance	Good precision with guidance needed	Poor precision with guidance needed	No attempt made	
Quality of finished product (25pts Max)	Final appearance of prepared tomato sauce with quality work achieved.	Excellent quality finished sauce, well presented.	Very good quality finished sauce, well presented.	Good quality finished sauce.	Poor quality finished product.	No attempt made	

Chapter Summary

The theme of this chapter is to understand how food is thawed, cooked, cooled, and later reheated safely. Highly susceptible populations must be given special consideration as prescribed in the food code, especially when serving raw or undercooked animal food.

Although there are a lot of temperatures listed in this chapter, many of them relate closely to the temperature danger zone. The following is a simplification of the temperatures and times covered.

Temperature danger zone:

- Temperature danger zone: 41°F – 135°F (5°C – 57°C).
- Bacterial growth maximized: 70°F – 125°F (21°C – 52°C)

Thawing highlights:

- Never thawed at room temperature
- No portion of a thawing TCS food may rise above 41°F (5°C) for more than 4 hours
- Microwave thawing must be followed by immediate cooking

Cooking highlights:

Plant foods	135°F (57°C)	Instantaneous
Seafood, steak	145°F (63°C)	15 seconds
Burgers, large birds	155°F (68°C)	17 seconds
Poultry, wild game	165°F (73°C)	Instantaneous

Cooling highlights (see example on next page):

- From 135°F to 70°F (57°C to 21°C) within 2 hours, *and*
- To 41°F (5°C) or below within 6 hours total

Reheating highlights:

- Reheat from 41°F to 165°F (5°C to 74°C) within 2 hours
- Hold at 165°F (74°C) for 15 seconds

Cooling Temperature Log

The Food Code requires that foods not cooked for immediate service be cooled quickly to minimize time in the temperature danger zone and limit bacterial growth. The specific time and temperature requirements are as follows:

- Cool to 70°F (21°C) within 2 hours
- Cool to 41°F (5°C) within an additional 4 hours.

Cooling Temperature Log									
Date	Initials	Food Product	Cooling Time/Temperature						Corrective Action
			Final Temp	Time	2 Hrs	Time	4 Hrs	Time	
1–1–23	ΔθΣ	Λασαγνα	155Φ (68°X)	8 αμ	70°Φ (21°X)	10 αμ	41°Φ (5°X)	12:00 πμ	
1–1–23	ΔθΣ	Βακεδ Ζιτι	155Φ (68°X)	8 αμ	90°Φ (32°X)				Δισχαρδεδ

Chapter 9W

Food Service

Once the food is properly cooked, reheated, or cooled (as covered in the previous chapter) it may be held for service until needed. Time/temperature for safety (TCS) food must be properly managed to prevent bacterial growth that can lead to foodborne illness.

Presenting food to a consumer is the last step in the flow of food. At this point the servers have specific requirements to prevent food and beverage contamination just before and while the consumer has the food in their possession. Food employees must carefully monitor self-service areas such as buffets and salad bars as well.

Finally, most of these food code requirements apply to off-site activities such as catered events or temporary food establishments. In fact, there are additional rules designed to keep food safe while being transported or served in an outdoor environment.

Key Terms
Keep an eye out for these essential topics:

- Hot & cold holding for service
- Time as a Public Health Control
- Tableware
- Multi-use to-go containers
- Catering
- Mobile units
- Temporary food establishments
- Vending machines

Objectives
After working through this chapter, you should be able to explain the following to friends and family:

- Understand the reason for hot and cold holding requirements
- Learn about holding without temperature control
- Explore the requirements for setting a table
- Understand the safety protocols for self-service areas
- Learn about the off-site operations and requirements
- Explain the safety requirements for vending machines

Recipe

Recipe: Béchamel Sauce

Béchamel sauce is another of our five mother sauces. It is a thick creamy white colored sauce. It is another basic sauce in which we can add one or more extra ingredients, to create a derivative sauce, which we will use in many different dishes. It is a building block, much like the chicken stock we produced in chapter 4 and the tomato sauce in chapter 8. We will make this Béchamel sauce, chill and freeze it, with the plan to use it with other components to make a meal later. In other words, we are making this sauce as part of our later mise en place.

Ingredients:

- 50g butter
- 50g flour
- 500ml milk
- 1/8 studded onion
- pinch nutmeg
- For Mornay add 50g cheese

Section 1

Reading assignment:

Read pages 185-191 in the coursebook, and then complete the activities below.

Fill in the missing words:

_____ growth is optimal when TCS food is in the _____ _____ _____, so the Food Code has specific requirements the food safety manager must adhere to when _____ food for service.

Questions:

What temperature range is bacterial growth maximized?

  a) 70-125 Fahrenheit (21-52 Celsius)
  b) 41-135 Fahrenheit (5-57 Celsius)
  c) 135-165 Fahrenheit (57-74 Celsius)
  d) 165-195 Fahrenheit (74-91 Celsius)

Cold food starting at 41 Fahrenheit (5 Celsius) or below, which never rises above 70 Fahrenheit (21 Celsius) can be served for how many hours?

  a. 2 hours
  b. 4 hours
  c. 5 hours
  d. 6 hours

A hot holding unit on a buffet must maintain the food to a minimum temperature of what?

  a. 135 Fahrenheit (57Celsius)
  b. 145 Fahrenheit (63Celsius)
  c. 155 Fahrenheit (68Celsius)
  d. 165 Fahrenheit (74Celsius)

TCS (Time & Temperature Controlled for Safety) foods must be temperature controlled at all times to maintain them outside of the TDZ (Temperature Danger Zone). Which of the following foods are TCS foods?

  a. Fresh chicken
  b. Sliced tomatoes
  c. Non-heat treated oil & garlic mixtures
  d. All of the above

Activity

Students will work in teams. There will need to be as many teams as there are options of cooling liquids. With the knowledge you already have, the equipment available and using the list below as a reminder, each team should heat exactly 1 gallon of tap water (with nothing added) to the boiling point 212 Fahrenheit (100°C). The water should then be put through the chosen cooling method for each team. Record how long it takes for the water to hit the top of the temperature danger zone 135 Fahrenheit and until it reaches room temperature, 70 Fahrenheit. The water can then be placed into the refrigerator and cooled to 41 Fahrenheit or below. You may not have time in your class to get this completed with every cooling method. That should be recorded, as it is valuable data.

Cooling methods:

- First should be the control. This pot should be heated and just turned off, the lid left on top, and with no cooling assistance given.

- Poured into a wide plastic container

- Poured into a wide metal container

- Add ice to the container (no more than ¼ gallon)

- Use a frozen ice paddle

- Place into an ice and water bath

- Place into a blast chiller

Cooling analysis Chart

Cooling method chosen	Time at boiling 212 Fahrenheit	Time at 135 Fahrenheit	Time at 70 Fahrenheit	Time at 41 Fahrenheit	Total time to get out of the TDZ
Control, not cooling assistance					
Poured into a wide plastic container					
Poured into a wide metal container					
Add ice to the container (no more than ¼ gallon)					
Use a frozen ice paddle					
Place into an ice and water bath					
Place into a blast chiller					

Section 2

Reading Assignment:

Read pages 192-201 in the coursebook, and then complete the activities below.

Fill in the missing words:

The FDA Food Code applies to all _____ _____ as the definition of a food establishment which includes a restaurant, delivery (i.e., bulk transportation), _____, temporary venues, mobile units, and _____ _____.

Questions:

A food establishment, which must obey all the FDA Food Code (within local laws) can include which of the following?

    a.   Restaurant

    b.   Catered or feeding location

    c.   Food bank

    d.   Vending location

Time and Temperature Controlled for Safety (TCS) foods must be consumed or disposed of in how many days?

    a.   3 days, including the date they were opened

    b.   5 days, including the date they were opened

    c.   7 days, including the date they were opened

    d.   10 days, including the date they were opened

When preparing for a catering event, which of the following isn't a legal requirement?

    a.   Electrical power

    b.   Potable water

    c.   Sewage Disposal

    d.   NSF certified equipment

What kind of program must be in place to avoid intentional contamination on a catered event?

    a.   Catering licensure program

    b.   Food defense program

    c.   USDA food safety program

    d.   DHEC food program

Activity:

Using all the data collected from the class, work out which was the best and rank the methods from best to worst.

-Have a discussion in your groups to discuss your findings.

-Was there anything that could be done differently to improve the results?

Section 3

Read the béchamel sauce recipe carefully and list all known Time & Temperature Control for Safety (TCS) ingredients.

Video Assignment:

Watch the béchamel sauce video carefully and note any new skills needed.

Activity:

With your team, make a plan for what ingredients you can prepare for your mise en place. Make any needed alterations due to the availability of products. Your team will also need to choose which cooling method is best, once the sauce is created. Bear in mind which will cool fastest, but protect the integrity of the sauce too.

In the Kitchen:

- Measure & weigh the raw ingredients for your team's sauce. Depending on available time, you may prepare the studded onion.
- Wrap and label all ingredients and store them appropriately.
- Create and record your equipment mise en place list with your team to be ready for tomorrow's practical.

Section 4

Prepare the béchamel sauce with your team. Read the grading rubric, to achieve the maximum points available.

In the Kitchen:

Each team creates their mise en place for the sauce (preparation of ingredients & equipment needed).

The team will follow the recipe. Create the sauce with any assistance needed from the instructor or the preparation video. Follow all steps in the recipe to successfully create the sauce. Make sure to lightly season the sauce, as you will be adding additional ingredients later.

Your team will need to rapidly cool the sauce to safe levels (70 Fahrenheit or lower) before placing into the refrigerator. Record the time that it takes to achieve refrigerator temperature below.

Cooling method chosen:

Time at boiling point 212 Fahrenheit:

Time at 135 Fahrenheit (TDZ):

Time at 70 Fahrenheit (TDZ):

Time at 41 Fahrenheit (TDZ):

Overall cooling time to cool out of the TDZ:

Wash, rinse & sanitize all equipment and tables used, completing this as a team.

Section 5

Team Presentation:

Each team should heat a small portion of their sauce and examine any differences between them. Taste the different sauces and take note how variances in cooking can influence the outcome.

Note below what you would do differently next time to change or enhance the recipe:

_____

_____

_____

_____

Watch and participate in the end-of-chapter review video.

Activity:

Recipe Cost Sheet: Students can now work out the recipe cost sheet and then discover the per-portion price.

_____

_____

_____

_____

_____

_____

_____

_____

_____

_____

_____

_____

_____

_____

_____

_____

_____

_____

_____

Recipe Cost Worksheet

Name:_____ Date: _____

Menu Item	
Number of Portions	**Portion Size**

Ingredient	Purchase Unit	Purchase cost	Unit cost	Amount Needed	Ingredient Cost

Total recipe cost	
Number of portions from recipe	
Portion Cost	

[Blank Page]

Grading Rubric- Cooling Methods

Students will use their knowledge and skills to precisely conduct an investigation into the best cooling methods available with the equipment that is available.

Students will be offered adequate time to complete this task, with scrutiny on their written information, safety and sanitation knowledge, accuracy, attractiveness and the quality of their finished document.

Safety and accuracy are key to your success.

Culinary Arts
Cooling Methods Rubric

Student name _____   Date _____

Category	Specifications	Highly Skilled (Professional) 25 pts	Skilled (First Cook) 20 pts	Moderately Skilled (Commis) 15pts	Low skilled 10pts (Developing)	No Attempt 0pts	Comments
Written information 25pts	All written information is spelled correctly and is accurate	No guidance needed with all written information being accurate	Minimal guidance needed with all written information being accurate	Some guidance needed with all written information being accurate	Substantial guidance needed with all written information being accurate	No attempt made	
Safety & Sanitation 25pts	Correct information according to regulatory authority rules is presented	Exemplary standards maintained with no guidance	Very good standards maintained with some guidance	Good standards maintained, needed guidance	Poor standards maintained, needed guidance	No attempt made	
Accuracy of overall document 25pts	Quality & precision of work, with accuracy of information	Excellent precision with no guidance	Very good precision with some guidance	Good precision with guidance needed	Poor precision with guidance needed	No attempt made	
Quality of finished document 25pts	Final appearance of prepared document with quality work achieved	Excellent quality finished poster, well presented	Very good quality finished poster, well presented	Good quality finished poster	Poor quality finished products	No attempt made	

Grading Rubric- Cheesy Béchamel Sauce

Students will see the video example, safely, professionally and accurately replicating the béchamel sauce.

Students will be offered adequate time to complete this task, with scrutiny on their safety and sanitation, accuracy, attractiveness and the quality of their finished product.

Students should ensure all equipment and work surfaces are cleaned, sanitized and stored.

Safety and accuracy are key to your success.

Culinary Arts
Cheesy Béchamel Sauce Recipe Rubric

Student name _____   Date _____

Category	Specifications	Highly Skilled (Professional) 25 pts	Skilled (First Cook) 20 pts	Moderately Skilled (Commis) 15pts	Low skilled 10pts (Developing)	No Attempt 0pts	Comments
Accuracy reading & following the recipe (25pts Max)	Reading, comprehending & following the recipe is done with accuracy	No guidance needed with reading, comprehending & following the recipe.	Minimal guidance needed with reading, comprehending & following the recipe.	Some guidance needed with reading, comprehending & following the recipe	Substantial guidance needed with reading, comprehending & following the recipe	No attempt made	
Safety & Sanitation (25pts Max)	Correctly following all regulatory authority rules when preparing foods.	Exemplary standards maintained with no guidance	Very good standards maintained with some guidance	Good standards maintained, needed guidance	Poor standards maintained, needed guidance	No attempt made	
Accuracy & precision of preparations (25pts Max)	Accuracy & precision of work, with knife cuts & preparations.	Excellent precision with no guidance	Very good precision with some guidance	Good precision with guidance needed	Poor precision with guidance needed	No attempt made	
Quality of finished product (25pts Max)	Final appearance of prepared Béchamel Sauce with quality work achieved.	Excellent quality finished sauce, well presented.	Very good quality finished sauce, well presented.	Good quality finished sauce.	Poor quality finished product.	No attempt made	

Chapter Summary

The theme of this chapter is to understand how food makes it from the kitchen to the consumer. Sometimes it happens immediately, but other times it may need to be delivered or held for service until needed. The hot and cold holding requirements are meant to prevent bacterial growth and keep food safe.

When food is served away from the primary food establishment, most of the food code is applicable. In fact, there are additional requirements to keep food safe from the less controlled surroundings.

Temperature danger zone:

- Temperature danger zone: 41°F – 135°F (5°C – 57°C).
- Bacterial growth maximized: 70°F – 125°F (21°C – 52°C)

Hot holding for service:

- Maintain hot food at 135°F (57°C) or above
- Exception: Properly cooked roasts may be held at 130°F (54°C) or above

Cold holding for service:

- Maintain cold food at 41°F (5°C) or below
- Frozen food must remain frozen

Time as a Public Health Control (TPHC):

<u>Hot food held without temperature control</u>

- Hot food starting at 135°F (57°C) or above may be held up to **4 hours** after it is removed from temperature control.

<u>Cold food held without temperature control</u>

- Cold food starting at 41°F (5°C) or below can be held up to **4 hours** after it is removed from temperature control if the temperature is not monitored.
- Cold food starting at 41°F (5°C) or below can be held up to **6 hours** after it is removed from temperature control if the temperature is monitored and never rises above 70°F (21°C).

[Blank Page]

Chapter 10W

Cleaning and Sanitizing

Cleaning and sanitizing are essential and required steps in a food establishment. A properly cleaned and sanitized food-contact surface or equipment is free of foreign particles and microorganisms, which could otherwise cause foodborne illness if consumed.

Cleaning and sanitizing are not the same thing. Cleaning removes the foreign particles, and sanitizing removes the microorganisms.

Most cleaning and sanitizing are proactive tasks and should be performed according to staff training and a master cleaning schedule. Some cleaning is reactive, such as someone getting sick and experiencing a sudden vomiting or diarrheal event.

Key Terms

Keep an eye out for these essential topics:

- Cleaning
- Sanitizing
- Food-contact surface
- Concentration
- Personal protective equipment (PPE)
- Water hardness
- Chlorine
- Iodine
- Quaternary ammonium (Quats)

Objectives

After working through this chapter, you should be able to explain the following to friends and family:

- Understand the difference between cleaning and sanitizing
- Learn about hot water sanitizing & chemical sanitizing
- Explore the requirements for dishwashing
- Understand how to protect clean items from contamination
- Describe the seriousness of responding to a sudden sickness
- Explain the time limits associated with cleaning equipment and utensils

Recipe

Recipe: Traditional Lasagna

We have now produced two mother sauces (tomato and béchamel) which we will combine with other ingredients to produce a full dish. We will need to safely defrost both sauces before we can make the traditional lasagna. This may need to be done days in advance, to allow complete defrosting in the safest manner, in the refrigerator. Lasagna is one of the oldest types of pasta, traditionally made into rectangular leaves. This is layered with a tomato meat sauce and topped with a creamy sauce and cheese, then baked in the oven. Depending on tastes and availability, the meat choices can be changed as well as making an entirely vegetarian version too.

Ingredients:

- 1 lb. lasagna noodles
- 1 tsp. olive oil
- 1.5 lb. ground beef
- 0.5 lb. Italian sausage
- salt & black pepper
- 1.5 pt tomato sauce
- 3 tsp ground garlic (into the tomato sauce)
- 2 tsp. dried oregano (into the tomato sauce)
- 1 pt. béchamel sauce
- 16 oz. grated cheese

Section 1

Reading assignment:

Read pages 205-210 in the coursebook, and then complete the activities below.

Fill in the missing words:

_____ is the process of removing visible organic matter and debris.

_____ is the process of destroying pathogenic microorganisms.

Questions:

Which of the following only needs to be cleaned and not sanitized?

a) Meat slicer
b) Knives
c) Cutting boards
d) Kitchen floor

Equipment and utensils used with TCS foods must be cleaned, at a minimum, every

a. 2 hours
b. 4 hours
c. 6 hours
d. Daily

Cooking & baking equipment must be cleaned at least every...

a. 4 hours
b. 6 hours
c. 12 hours
d. 24 hours

What caution should be taken with abrasive cleaners?

a. They don't clean well with hot water
b. They can leave surfaces scratched
c. They must be used with special brushes
d. They can't be rinsed down a municipal drain

Group Activity

It is time to take a look at the growth of your bread petri dish projects. As a class (without opening any of the bags and disturbing the gross growths) lay out the petri dishes and study the colors and shapes. Human beings cannot see individual microorganisms, but once they grow into colonies of millions we can see their mass. They exhibit different shapes of colonies, depending on their type and the space available for growth. One way we can make some basic identifications is through their color. Let's take a look and see what you may have.

Yellow – Staphylococcus Aureus (responsible for skin and other infections)
Blue/green - bacillus pyocyaneus (Skin & systemic infections)
Pale pink to deep red – Enterobacteriaceae colonies (Microbes often found in the gut)

Transparent — Salmonella (Gastrointestinal illness)

There is also a possibility that the colonies can be fungi colonies, which can include the following:

- Green/blue-green - Aspergillus genus
- Grey-turquoise - Aspergillus fumigatus
- Yellow-green of Aspergillus flavus
- Creamy-white of Aspergillus candidus
- Black - Aspergillus niger

Record below what colonies you see in the petri dishes. Briefly describe a professional description that you would give to train a fellow employee not to use their cellphone in the kitchen. As a "manager" you should describe both scientific and legal reasons.

Overall, hopefully, it has become very apparent the reasons why we are NOT allowed to handle our cellphones in the kitchen! Maybe it's time to get out the disinfectant wipes! (Please dispose of the petri dishes carefully to not disturb or open the packages. They aren't particularly nice!)

Section 2

Reading Assignment:

Read pages 211-221 in the coursebook, and then complete the activities below.

Fill in the missing words:

A cleaning solution _____ results from _____ a chemical cleaner with _____ following guidelines on the product label.

Questions:

How long is the required contact time for chlorine bleach to sanitize equipment?

    a.   7 seconds

    b.   30 seconds

    c.   1 minute

    d.   90 seconds

In a three pot sink cleaning system, what should the temperature be in the soapy detergent sink?

    a.   110 Fahrenheit 43 Celsius

    b.   120 Fahrenheit 49 Celsius

    c.   130 Fahrenheit 54 Celsius

    d.   140 Fahrenheit 60 Celsius

Which is the correct method of drying equipment?

    a.   Towel dry with a clean towel

    b.   Paper towels

    c.   Air dry in a self-draining position

    d.   Wiped with a clean sanitized cloth

Where should mops be stored?

    a.   Hanging above the mop sink

    b.   In the mop bucket

    c.   In a sanitizer solution

    d.   In clean water

Activity:

Read the lasagna recipe carefully and list all known Time & Temperature Control for Safety (TCS) ingredients.

Video Assignment:

Watch the lasagna video carefully and note any new skills needed.

Section 3

Activity:

With your team, make a plan for what ingredients you can prepare for your mise en place. Make any needed alterations due to preference of meats and availability of products. Your team will sear the ground meats today, as part of the mise en place. You will add the fully cooked meats directly to the tomato sauce and ensure it is heated to a minimum of 165 Fahrenheit. Your team will need to choose which cooling method is best, once the sauce is created. Bear in mind which will cool fastest, but protect the integrity of the sauce too.

In the Kitchen:

- Measure & weigh the raw ingredients for your team's lasagna.
- As previously mentioned, prepare and cook the tomato meat sauce.
- Wrap and label all ingredients and store them appropriately.
- Create and record your equipment mise en place list with your team to be ready for tomorrow's practical.

Section 4

Prepare the lasagna dish with your team. Read the grading rubric, to achieve the maximum points available.

In the Kitchen:

Each team creates their mise en place for the lasagna (preparation of ingredients & equipment needed).

The team will follow the recipe. Create the lasagna with any assistance needed from the instructor or the preparation video. Follow all steps in the recipe to successfully create the sauce. Make sure to taste each component to ensure it is correctly seasoned, before they are married together into the finished dish.

Your team will need to rapidly cool the lasagna to safe levels (70 Fahrenheit or lower) before placing into the refrigerator. Your team will need to agree on the best method to cool the finished product, without damaging its integrity.

Wash, rinse & sanitize all equipment and tables used, completing this as a team.

Section 5

Team Presentation:

Each team should heat a portion of their lasagna and examine any differences between them. Taste the different lasagnas and take note how variances in cooking can influence the outcome.

Note below what you would do differently next time to change or enhance the recipe:

_____

_____

_____

Activity:

Recipe Cost Sheet: Students can now work out the recipe cost sheet and then discover the per-portion price.

Watch and participate in the end-of-chapter review video.

_____

_____

_____

_____

_____

_____

_____

_____

_____

_____

_____

_____

_____

_____

_____

_____

_____

_____

_____

_____

Recipe Cost Worksheet

Name:_____ Date: _____

Menu Item	
Number of Portions	**Portion Size**

Ingredient	Purchase Unit	Purchase cost	Unit cost	Amount Needed	Ingredient Cost

Total recipe cost	
Number of portions from recipe	
Portion Cost	

[Blank Page]

Grading Rubric- Reading the Bread Petri Dishes

Students will use their knowledge and skills to precisely conduct an investigation into the results of their bread petri dishes. They will also create a statement on the reasons why cellphone usage in the kitchen is not acceptable.

Students will be offered adequate time to complete this task, with scrutiny on their written information, safety and sanitation knowledge, accuracy, attractiveness and the quality of their finished document.

Safety and accuracy are key to your success.

Culinary Arts

Bread Petri Dishes Analysis Rubric

Student name _____ Date _____

Category	Specifications	Highly Skilled (Professional) 25 pts	Skilled (First Cook) 20 pts	Moderately Skilled (Commis) 15pts	Low skilled 10pts (Developing)	No Attempt 0pts	Comments
Written information 25pts	All written information is spelled correctly and is accurate	No guidance needed with all written information being accurate	Minimal guidance needed with all written information being accurate	Some guidance needed with all written information being accurate	Substantial guidance needed with all written information being accurate	No attempt made	
Safety & Sanitation 25pts	Correct information according to regulatory authority rules is presented	Exemplary standards maintained with no guidance	Very good standards maintained with some guidance	Good standards maintained, needed guidance	Poor standards maintained, needed guidance	No attempt made	
Accuracy of overall document 25pts	Quality & precision of work, with accuracy of information	Excellent precision with no guidance	Very good precision with some guidance	Good precision with guidance needed	Poor precision with guidance needed	No attempt made	
Quality of finished document 25pts	Final appearance of prepared document with quality work achieved	Excellent quality finished document, well presented	Very good quality finished document, well presented	Good quality finished document	Poor quality finished document	No attempt made	

Grading Rubric- Lasagna

Students will see the video example, safely, professionally and accurately replicating the lasagna.

Students will be offered adequate time to complete this task, with scrutiny on their safety and sanitation, accuracy, attractiveness and the quality of their finished product.

Students should ensure all equipment and work surfaces are cleaned, sanitized and stored.

Safety and accuracy are key to your success.

Culinary Arts
Lasagna Recipe Rubric

Student name _____   Date _____

Category	Specifications	Highly Skilled (Professional) 25 pts	Skilled (First Cook) 20 pts	Moderately Skilled (Commis) 15pts	Low skilled 10pts (Developing)	No Attempt 0pts	Comments
Accuracy reading & following the recipe (25pts Max)	Reading, comprehending & following the recipe is done with accuracy	No guidance needed with reading, comprehending & following the recipe.	Minimal guidance needed with reading, comprehending & following the recipe.	Some guidance needed with reading, comprehending & following the recipe	Substantial guidance needed with reading, comprehending & following the recipe	No attempt made	
Safety & Sanitation (25pts Max)	Correctly following all regulatory authority rules when preparing foods.	Exemplary standards maintained with no guidance	Very good standards maintained with some guidance	Good standards maintained, needed guidance	Poor standards maintained, needed guidance	No attempt made	
Accuracy & precision of preparations (25pts Max)	Accuracy & precision of work, with knife cuts & preparations.	Excellent precision with no guidance	Very good precision with some guidance	Good precision with guidance needed	Poor precision with guidance needed	No attempt made	
Quality of finished product (25pts Max)	Final appearance of prepared lasagna with quality work achieved.	Excellent quality finished lasagna, well presented.	Very good quality finished lasagna, well presented.	Good quality finished lasagna.	Poor quality finished product.	No attempt made	

Chapter Summary

Cleaning and sanitizing food-contact surfaces, equipment, and utensils are essential to keeping food safe and preventing foodborne illness. A manager must understand the requirements, have a written plan, and be prepared to describe the standard operating procedures (SOP) to an inspector. Corrective actions should be taken, and retaining is given when staff is observed not cleaning and sanitizing correctly or at the required frequency.

Working with chemical sanitizers can be dangerous if mishandled or not used according to their instruction. Staff should have training and access to personal protective equipment (PPE).

Cleaning and sanitizing frequency:

- TCS food-contact surfaces: Every 4 hours or less
- Non-TCS food-contact surfaces: Every 24 hours or less

Basic cleaning and sanitizing steps:

- Washing
- Rinsing
- Sanitizing
- Air drying

Liquid temperatures:

<u>Hot water only</u>
- Hot water/heat sanitizing: 171°F (77°C) for 30 seconds
- Dishwashing machine: 180°F (82°C) or 165°F (74°C) for stationary racks

<u>Water + chemical solution:</u>
- Manual dishwashing: 110°F (43°C) or higher

Chemical concentrations:

- Chlorine   50-99 ppm,   7 seconds
- Iodine   12.5 – 25 ppm,   30 seconds
- Quats   Per manufacturer, 30 seconds, water hardness: 500 ppm or less

[Blank Page]

Chapter 11W

Facility and Equipment

A restaurant cannot be successful or comply with the Food Code with inadequate equipment or an improperly designed and maintained facility.

A properly designed facility involves professional architects, engineers, foodservice consultants, and building and health officials. Careful planning and review go into developing the plans and specifications long before the construction teams start their work. This includes ensuring the building systems can support the intended use, including water pressure, hot water capacity, HVAC and ventilation, and electrical capacity and lighting intensity.

The equipment selection and investment are equally important. The equipment must be approved, durable, and easy to clean. Selecting the wrong equipment or trying to save money on a less powerful or lower-capacity item will lead to lower productivity and potentially underperforming food quality — maybe not unsafe but not satisfactory to the customer. Loss of revenue occurs when equipment needs to be prematurely replaced due to failure or an item does not meet the needs of an operation.

Key Terms

Keep an eye out for these essential topics:

- Construction documents
- Permit to operate
- Easily cleanable
- Cross-connection
- Backflow prevention
- Counter-mounted equipment
- American National Standards Institute (ANSI)
- NSF International

Objectives

After working through this chapter, you should be able to explain the following to friends and family:

- Appreciate the process necessary to design a restaurant
- Learn about a permit to operate and a certificate of occupancy
- Explore the facilities construction and material requirements
- Understand the required light intensity levels
- Describe the basic building systems (HVAC, electrical, and plumbing)
- Explain the installation requirements for food equipment

Recipe

Recipe: Focaccia Bread

Focaccia bread is an Italian-style, high-hydration bread. It can be used to create delicious sandwiches, pizzas, and flatbreads. The words "high hydration" indicates its significant water content. This creates a tacky texture and delicate dough that must not be overworked. The dough is coated in olive oil, to create an incredibly rich but fresh flavor. This creates a very light and fluffy bread with a slightly seared edge, from the oil content.

Ingredients:

- 5g yeast
- 350ml very warm water
- 390g bread flour
- 8g salt
- 83g olive oil (2/3 for recipe, 1/3 topping)
- optional toppings like cheeses, caramelized onion, pizza toppings, etc.

Section 1

Reading assignment:

Read pages 225-233 in the coursebook, and then complete the activities below.

Fill in the missing words:

When the state, county, city, or tribal _____ _____ has adopted the FDA Food Code, it adheres to safeguard public health and ensure that food is safe, unadulterated, and _____ _____ when offered to the consumer. These requirements, along with building codes and zoning regulations, directly influence the design of the building and, subsequently, the _____ _____ _____.

Questions:

During construction, a new restaurant is closed off to just the contractor and those designated to be on the site. What is issued prior to the owner being able to move into the space and start operating?

   a) Occupancy Permission Slip
   b) Contractor Designation papers
   c) Certificate of Occupancy
   d) Operator Credibility Certificate

Which of the following are required storage spaces?

   a. Garbage
   b. Hazardous materials
   c. Contaminated or recalled products
   d. All of the above

Which of the following is NOT a true statement about staff breakrooms?

   a. Staff breakrooms are required to have a location for employment posters.
   b. Staff breakrooms are required to give staff a minimum of 1 hour off every 5 hours of work.
   c. Staff breakrooms are mandated to have a training facility on the premises.
   d. Staff breakrooms are not required but are a good practice.

It is imperative that floors, walls, and ceilings must be smooth, durable, and

_____.

   a. Re-paintable
   b. Easily cleanable
   c. Replicable
   d. Stainless steel coated

Activity

Design your own "The Big 6" Pathogens chart of the most common bad bugs with your new knowledge, and from any further research you do. Your poster should have the name, a likeness to the pathogen and one fact about the bad bug, like common places it is found. Ensure all wording is correct and easily legible. See the example below, and remember to keep designs simple and add some color, if available. Read the rubric to achieve the best grade.

Section 2

Reading Assignment:

Read pages 233-241 in the coursebook, and then complete the activities below.

Fill in the missing words:

Each handwashing sink or group of handwashing sinks must have:

1. Hand cleaning liquid, powder, or bar _____ (one per two sinks minimum)

2. _____ _____ provisions

3. _____ receptacle (if disposable towels are used)

4. _____ signage (one per sink)

Questions:

Coved edges on flooring are important in the facility. What does it do?

   a. Provides a smooth transition between the flooring & walls, to aid cleaning.
   b. Helps highlight trapped dirt to the health inspector.
   c. Offers a cove to minimize water seepage behind the walls.
   d. Helps retain moisture to add humidity to the dry kitchen environment.

All openings to the outside must be protected. What is a commonly used method?

   a. Shutting the front door.
   b. Close windows at dusk, as flying insects tend to be attracted to the lights in the kitchen.
   c. The use of window screens, to stop insect entry.
   d. All of the above.

The outdoor garbage (refuse) area must have a curb built around the perimeter and a sloped floor surface. Why?

   a. To stop the dumpsters from rolling away unintentionally
   b. It helps the refuse to be efficiently and safely removed by the appropriate dumpster trucks.
   c. It ensures any leaks from the dumpsters are contained until the refuse is collected.

Which of the following are considered to be approved water sources?

   a. A public water system
   b. A private water system
   c. Water transport vehicles
   d. All of the above

Activity:

Complete your "The Big 6" pathogens poster and submit it for a vote with the class. The best posters can be displayed in the kitchen or classroom. Your poster should have the name, a likeness to the pathogen and one fact about the bad bug, like common places it is found.

Section 3

Read the focaccia bread recipe carefully and list all known Time & Temperature Control for Safety (TCS) ingredients.

Video Assignment:

Watch the focaccia bread video carefully and note any new skills needed.

Activity:

With your team, make a plan for what ingredients you can prepare for your mise en place. Make any needed or desired alterations to the recipe, as the bread can have many toppings and seasonings added. Keep it fairly simple, to keep it tasty!

In the Kitchen:

- Measure & weigh the raw ingredients for your team's bread dough. Measure the needed water on the day you cook. Depending on your available class time, your team may need to prepare and cook some toppings.

- Wrap and label all ingredients and store them appropriately.

- Create and record your equipment mise en place list with your team to prepare for tomorrow's lab.

Section 4

Prepare the focaccia bread dough with a team. Read the grading rubric, to achieve the maximum points available.

In the Kitchen:

Each team creates its mise en place for the focaccia bread dough (preparation of ingredients & equipment needed).

The team will follow the recipe. Create the bread dough with any assistance needed from the instructor or the preparation video. The dough will then be retarded in the refrigerator overnight and completed and baked the following day.

Each team should wash, rinse, and sanitize their equipment and work surfaces to the standards shown in the video and discussed in the coursebook.

Recipe Cost Sheet:

Students will start to work out the recipe cost sheet and then complete the per-portion price. This will be completed tomorrow, once the bread is baking.

Section 5

In the Kitchen:

Each team will take the bread from the refrigerator, allow it to warm, so the yeast becomes active again. It can then be shaped and topped with the chosen toppings.

The team will follow the recipe. Create the bread dough with any assistance needed from the instructor or the preparation video.

Each team should wash, rinse, and sanitize their equipment and work surfaces to the standards shown in the video and discussed in the coursebook.

Recipe Cost Sheet:

Once the bread is baking and the team has cleaned the kitchen, students will complete the recipe cost sheet (on the next page) and then complete the per-portion price.

Team presentation:

Each team will present a small amount of their focaccia bread to the other teams. The teams will inspect each of the creations and analyze the results.

Watch and participate in the end-of-chapter review video.

Recipe Cost Sheet: Focaccia Bread

Name:_____ Date: _____

Menu Item	
Number of Portions	**Portion Size**

Ingredient	Purchase Unit	Purchase cost	Unit cost	Amount Needed	Ingredient Cost

Total recipe cost	
Number of portions from recipe	
Portion Cost	

[Blank Page]

The "BIG 6" Pathogens Grading Rubric

Students will see an example and professionally and accurately replicate the six pathogens, arranging them in a visually easy to understand way and grouping them to maximize memory retention.

Students will be offered adequate time to complete this task, with scrutiny on their written information, safety and sanitation, accuracy, attractiveness and the quality of their finished product.

It is recommended that students use simple drawn examples to keep the information clear. Add some color to your work; a bold poster is eye appealing and will be more successful in educating others when on display.

Safety and accuracy are key to your success.

Student name _____   Date _____

Culinary Arts
Big 6 Poster Rubric

Category	Specifications	Highly Skilled (Professional) 25 pts	Skilled (First Cook) 20 pts	Moderately Skilled (Commis) 15pts	Low Skilled 10pts (Developing)	No Attempt 0pts	Comments
Written information 25pts	All written information is spelled correctly and is accurate	No guidance needed with all written information being accurate	Minimal guidance needed with all written information being accurate	Some guidance needed with all written information being accurate	Substantial guidance needed with all written information being accurate	No attempt made	
Safety & Sanitation 25pts	Correct information according to regulatory authority rules is presented	Exemplary standards maintained with no guidance	Very good standards maintained with some guidance	Good standards maintained, needed guidance	Poor standards maintained, needed guidance	No attempt made	
Accuracy of overall poster 25pts	Quality & precision of work, with accuracy of images and overall poster	Excellent precision with no guidance	Very good precision with some guidance	Good precision with guidance needed	Poor precision with guidance needed	No attempt made	
Quality of finished product 25pts	Final appearance of prepared poster with quality work achieved	Excellent quality finished poster, well presented	Very good quality finished poster, well presented	Good quality finished poster	Poor quality finished products	No attempt made	

Focaccia Bread Rubric

Students will see the video example, safely, professionally, and accurately replicating the focaccia bread.

Students will be offered adequate time to complete this task, with scrutiny on their safety and sanitation, accuracy, attractiveness, and quality of their finished product.

Students should ensure all equipment and work surfaces are cleaned, sanitized and stored.

Safety and accuracy are key to your success.

Culinary Arts
Focaccia Bread Recipe Rubric

Student name _____   Date _____

Category	Specifications	Highly Skilled (Professional) 25 pts	Skilled (First Cook) 20 pts	Moderately Skilled (Commis) 15pts	Low skilled 10pts (Developing)	No Attempt 0pts	Comments
Accuracy reading & following the recipe (25pts Max)	Reading, comprehending & following the recipe is done with accuracy	No guidance needed with reading, comprehending & following the recipe.	Minimal guidance needed with reading, comprehending & following the recipe.	Some guidance needed with reading, comprehending & following the recipe	Substantial guidance needed with reading, comprehending & following the recipe	No attempt made	
Safety & Sanitation (25pts Max)	Correctly following all regulatory authority rules when preparing foods.	Exemplary standards maintained with no guidance	Very good standards maintained with some guidance	Good standards maintained, needed guidance	Poor standards maintained, needed guidance	No attempt made	
Accuracy & precision of preparations (25pts Max)	Accuracy & precision of work, with knife cuts & preparations.	Excellent precision with no guidance	Very good precision with some guidance	Good precision with guidance needed	Poor precision with guidance needed	No attempt made	
Quality of finished product (25pts Max)	Final appearance of prepared Focaccia Bread with quality work achieved.	Excellent quality finished bread, well presented.	Very good quality finished bread, well presented.	Good quality finished bread.	Poor quality finished product.	No attempt made	

Chapter Summary

A well-designed and properly maintained food operation, with approved and quality equipment, are the ingredients for a successful business that can comply with the Food Code requirements. This all starts with a professional design team and the production of drawings and specifications, followed by a building and health inspector review. The final approved project receives a certificate of occupancy and a permit to operate as a food establishment.

The building systems must be able to accommodate the demand of the operation, from water pressure and temperature to adequate ventilation and plumbing to electrical capacity and lighting intensities. Additionally, the water supply must be from an approved source, protected from contamination with backflow prevention, and never allow a cross-connection to any other system.

The foodservice equipment must be from an ANSI accredited program, such as NSF International, which independently tests and approves food preparation equipment for safe use and cleanability. Approved equipment should bear the NSF label.

Chapter numbers review:

- Water temperature at a handwashing sink: 100°F to 108°F (38°C - 42°C).
- Light intensity levels: 10, 20, and 50 fc (108, 215, and 540 lux)
- Maximum equipment spacing from adjacent walls/equipment: 1/32" (1 mm)
- Equipment height:
    - 6" (15 cm) above a floor
    - 4" (10 cm) above a countertop

[Blank Page]

Chapter 12W
Pest Control

In addition to the fact that customers do not like seeing insects or rodents while dining, these tiny creatures carry disease and can contaminate food and food-contact surfaces. Steps must be taken to minimize their presence.

Understanding the various pests to watch out for and how they find their way into a facility is required in order to effectively monitor and control their activity. Additionally, outdoor areas such as dining or trash storage areas require special attention as well.

When pests show, a prepared plan must be enacted to safely manage the problem in and around food. This requires an integrated pest management (IPM) plan and will benefit from a professional pest control operator (PCO). When using and storing toxic chemicals on the premises, there are some specific rules to follow for employee safety and consumer health.

Key Terms
Keep an eye out for these essential topics:

- Pests
- Service animal
- Infestation
- Air curtain
- Sealed
- Integrated Pest Management (IPM)
- Pest control operator (PCO)
- Pesticide

Objectives
After working through this chapter, you should be able to explain the following to friends and family:

- Learn about the kinds of pests to watch for
- Explore the problem areas inside and outside an operation
- Understand how to create an integrated pest management (IPM) program
- Describe the benefits of working with a pest control operator (PCO)
- Explain the storage and use requirements related to poisonous and toxic materials

Recipe

Recipe: One Pot Chicken & Rice Dinner

This method will be putting a combination cooking method to the test. We will start off dry with a little oil, sweating the vegetables, then add the chicken to sear it off, followed by the rice. By coating the rice in the oil, it will remain light and fluffy and not clump together once finished. We then add in some of our fresh chicken stock to add moisture to our cooking method. With a gentle simmer, we can enjoy a delicious, nutritious meal, that only took one pot to cook it in.

Ingredients:

- 1/3 cup vegetable oil
- ½ cup chopped carrots
- ½ cup chopped celery
- 1 cup chopped onion
- salt and pepper
- 2 cups long grain white rice
- 3 cups fresh chicken stock (pull out of the freezer in advance)
- 1lb chicken breast (cut into bite sized pieces)
- ¼ cup quinoa (washed, simmered for 5 minutes and drained)

Section 1

Reading assignment:

Read pages 245-250 in the coursebook, and then complete the activities below.

Fill in the missing words:

Many types of pests can cause problems for a food establishment. The most prevalent pest type can vary by _____ _____, type of food establishment, building construction, exterior lighting, and _____ _____. These small to microscopic living things can carry _____, infest stored products, as well as contaminate.

Questions:

What is the Food Code's catchall word to describe any undesirable and destructive insect or animal within the food operation?

    a) Pests
    b) Bugs
    c) Critters
    d) Living organisms

What are the most prevalent illnesses caused by rodent infestations?

    a. E. coli
    b. Salmonella
    c. Listeria
    d. All the above

How do flies consume solid foods?

    a. By chewing small amounts, as they only have small front teeth.
    b. By scraping small amounts with their feet, which have sharp hairs on them.
    c. By vomiting on it and sucking it up through their straw-shaped tongue.
    d. All of the above.

While pets are largely prohibited from food establishments (except in approved outdoor dining areas), service animals are an exception and are not considered pets. What law offers this protection?

    a. ADA
    b. FDA
    c. USDA
    d. DHEC

Class Activity: The Pest Game

Today we will create a game that we will be able to play tomorrow, to highlight challenges we deal with when it comes to pests in our establishment. It will help us to consider what issues we may face and what are the best and worst decisions we can make. It should be fun, so use a little imagination, too.

Each team has the task of creating idea cards (about the size of playing cards) to help the fun continue to move along.

Team 1 – Write as many different types (minimum of 6) of bugs we find infesting kitchens (roaches, spiders, palmetto bugs, ants etc.).

Team 2 – Write as many different types (minimum of 6) of rodents & other animals we find infesting kitchens (mice, rats, raccoons etc.).

Team 3 – Write as many different types (minimum of 6) of ways to kill pests. These can be professional or bad mistakes some people make (mouse traps, bug spray, approved rodenticide, fly paper).

Team 4 – Write as many different types (minimum of 6) of individuals who are trying to kill the pests (PCO--Pest Control Operator, sous chef, maître d', server etc.).

Section 2

Reading Assignment:

Read pages 250-255 in the coursebook, and then complete the activities below.

Fill in the missing words:

The Food Code prohibits the accumulation of _____ and unnecessary equipment inside and outside the food establishment to avoid attracting and creating _____ for insects and rodents. The overall upkeep and cleanliness of the operation are essential to preventing an _____, which is a significant number of pests established in a given area.

Questions:

How often should the outdoor trash area be cleaned?

    a.   Daily

    b.   After each trash collection

    c.   Twice monthly

    d.   Every 28 days

How many inches off the floor should products like food be stored?

    a.   4

    b.   6

    c.   8

    d.   12

What does PCO stand for?

    a.   Penetrating control ordinances

    b.   Pest Control organization

    c.   Pest Contract Operator

    d.   Pest Control Operator

What does SDS stand for?

    a.   Safety Data Sheets

    b.   Succinct Data Sheets

    c.   Safety Data Schedule

    d.   Safety Data Stance

Class Activity: The Pest Game

Today the class will all get together and have some fun. The four sets of cards should be in separate stacks on a central table. Every person in the classroom should play at least once, so their participation can be observed by the instructor and more importantly that everyone can have fun and learn the good and the bad mistakes that happen when it comes to pest control.

Each team should send one representative up for each round. The four individuals in each round will collect one card from one of the four stacks, so each round will have a bug, rodent or other animal, a way to kill the infestation, and who is doing it. Each student will create a sentence, including their item on their card. This should be a fast moving fun game. Here is an example:

*One evening, long long ago, a **cockroach** walked into a restaurant, looking for something to eat. At the back of the restaurant, a **raccoon** was looking for a snack and walked in the back door, sniffing the delicious goodies. The **cook** turned around and screamed as she saw a smiling raccoon, digging into the banana cream pie. She grabbed for the **bug spray**, slipped on the roach that scurried under her foot, and landed headfirst on the banana cream pie. The raccoon licked her unconscious face clean of the pie filling and scampered away into the night.*

As you complete each round, spend no more than 1 minute talking about mistakes made in each story. Then carry on to the next round. Have fun, laugh, and learn.

Section 3

Read the one pot chicken & rice dinner recipe carefully and list all known Time & Temperature Control for Safety (TCS) ingredients.

Video Assignment:

Watch the one pot chicken & rice dinner video carefully and note any new skills needed.

Activity:

With your team, make a plan for what ingredients you can prepare for your mise en place. Make any needed or desired alterations to the recipe, including meat or vegetables.

In the Kitchen:

- Measure & weigh the raw ingredients for your team's recipe. Make sure your chicken stock is defrosting safely. Depending on your available class time, your team may need to prepare and cook some ingredients.
- Wrap and label all ingredients and store them appropriately.
- Create and record your equipment mise en place list with your team to prepare for tomorrow's lab.

If you have time after cleaning your kitchen up, shuffle the cards and play some more rounds of The Pest Game.

Section 4

Prepare the one pot chicken & rice dinner with your team. Read the grading rubric, to achieve the maximum points available.

In the Kitchen:

Each team creates its mise en place for the one pot chicken & rice dinner (preparation of ingredients & equipment needed).

The team will follow the recipe. Create the recipe with any assistance needed from the instructor or the preparation video.

Each team should wash, rinse, and sanitize their equipment and work surfaces to the standards shown in the video and discussed in the course book.

Each team will share their results and compare their dish with the other teams. As you compare, discuss what the differences are and what made those differences.

Section 5

Recipe Cost Sheet:

Students will complete the recipe cost sheet and then complete the per-portion price.

Class Activity:

Shuffle the cards and play some more rounds of The Pest Game. By now, you should all be experts, coming up with unbelievable stories, but also recognizing what should be done to create a pest free environment.

Watch and participate in the end-of-chapter review video.

Recipe Cost Sheet: One Pot Chicken & Rice Dinner

Name:_____ Date: _____

Menu Item	
Number of Portions	Portion Size

Ingredient	Purchase Unit	Purchase cost	Unit cost	Amount Needed	Ingredient Cost

Total recipe cost	
Number of portions from recipe	
Portion Cost	

[Blank Page]

The Pest Game Grading Rubric

Students will see the example and using a little imagination and their newfound knowledge will create a line in the story, including your item on your flash card. This is designed to maximize memory retention.

Students will be offered adequate time to create the idea, with scrutiny on their written cards, safety and sanitation, accuracy, attractiveness, and the quality of their finished ideas. Remember, it's not about having a storyline that is healthy, but recognizing one that is not.

Together the whole class should be able to learn and feel very comfortable with the rules dictating pests and what we need to do to avoid them or get rid of them.

Safety and accuracy are key to your success.

Student name _____

Culinary Arts
The Pest Game Rubric

Date _____

Category	Specifications	Highly Skilled (Professional) 25 pts	Skilled (First Cook) 20 pts	Moderately Skilled (Commis) 15pts	Low Skilled 10pts (Developing)	No Attempt 0pts	Comments
Written information 25pts	All written information is spelled correctly and is accurate	No guidance needed with all written information being accurate	Minimal guidance needed with all written information being accurate	Some guidance needed with all written information being accurate	Substantial guidance needed with all written information being accurate	No attempt made	
Safety & Sanitation 25pts	Correct information according to regulatory authority rules is presented	Exemplary standards maintained with no guidance	Very good standards maintained with some guidance	Good standards maintained, needed guidance	Poor standards maintained, needed guidance	No attempt made	
Accuracy of overall sentences 25pts	Quality & precision of work, with accuracy of knowledge.	Excellent precision with no guidance	Very good precision with some guidance	Good precision with guidance needed	Poor precision with guidance needed	No attempt made	
Overall performance & participation 25pts	Final appearance of prepared flashcards/stories with quality work achieved	Excellent quality finished flashcards/stories well presented	Very good quality finished flashcards/stories well presented	Good quality finished flashcards/stories	Poor quality finished flashcards/stories	No attempt made	

One Pot Chicken & Rice Dinner Rubric

Students will see the video example, safely, professionally, and accurately replicating the dinner.

Students will be offered adequate time to complete this task, with scrutiny on their safety and sanitation, accuracy, attractiveness, and quality of their finished product.

Students should ensure all equipment and work surfaces are cleaned, sanitized and stored.

Safety and accuracy are key to your success.

Culinary Arts
One Pot Chicken & Rice Recipe Rubric

Student name _____   Date _____

Category	Specifications	Highly Skilled (Professional) 25 pts	Skilled (First Cook) 20 pts	Moderately Skilled (Commis) 15pts	Low skilled 10pts (Developing)	No Attempt 0pts	Comments
Accuracy reading & following the recipe (25pts Max)	Reading, comprehending & following the recipe is done with accuracy	No guidance needed with reading, comprehending & following the recipe.	Minimal guidance needed with reading, comprehending & following the recipe.	Some guidance needed with reading, comprehending & following the recipe	Substantial guidance needed with reading, comprehending & following the recipe	No attempt made	
Safety & Sanitation (25pts Max)	Correctly following all regulatory authority rules when preparing foods.	Exemplary standards maintained with no guidance	Very good standards maintained with some guidance	Good standards maintained, needed guidance	Poor standards maintained, needed guidance	No attempt made	
Accuracy & precision of preparations (25pts Max)	Accuracy & precision of work, with knife cuts & preparations.	Excellent precision with no guidance	Very good precision with some guidance	Good precision with guidance needed	Poor precision with guidance needed	No attempt made	
Quality of finished product (25pts Max)	Final appearance of prepared rice dish with quality work achieved.	Excellent quality finished rice dish, well presented.	Very good quality finished rice dish, well presented.	Good quality finished rice dish.	Poor quality finished product.	No attempt made	

Chapter Summary

In a food establishment, pests mustn't be allowed to enter or multiply within the facility easily. If they do, they pose a severe public health concern as food becomes contaminated and can result in foodborne illness or an allergic reaction when consumed.

An integrated pest management (IPM) program defines a process that monitors for pest activity and defines a timely response when an infestation is identified. Working with a professional pest control operator (PCO) is also beneficial to ensure safe and effective methods are used. Pesticides can be dangerous for employees to handle, and they can also contaminate food if carelessly misused.

Steps to properly manage pests:

- Eliminate all openings, cracks, and gaps in your building
- Inspect products at receiving for insects or rodents, including signs of activity or damage
- Store pesticides in their original packaging
- Apply pesticides only per the label
- Store pesticides separate from food and food-contact surfaces
- Hire a professional pest control operator (PCO) to apply pesticides
- Pets are prohibited from food production areas and largely prohibited from food service establishments (except dogs in approved outdoor dining areas)
- Fish aquariums and service animals for the disabled are permitted in customer areas only

[Blank Page]

Chapter 13W

Management Systems and Crisis Planning

Running a safe and successful operation does not happen by accident. It requires careful planning and staff training, all of which must be documented and recorded. The management systems employed must be based on sound scientific principles in order to be confident food will be protected against the primary risk factors associated with foodborne illness. With these management documents and records in hand, the food operation can confidently operate and easily pass inspections.

Management must also plan for a crisis, such as fire, flooding, loss of power, and more. Having a plan in place allows decisions to be made more quickly and with confidence. With a well-prepared crisis management plan, the food operation can keep staff and food safe if remaining open is possible. Being able to remain open during a crisis can be a significant benefit to the local community who may not be able to prepare food in their homes or have been required to evacuate.

Key Terms

Keep an eye out for these essential topics:

- Risk
- Person in Charge (PIC)
- Active Managerial Control
- HACCP
- Prerequisite programs
- Hazard
- Critical control point (CCP)
- Imminent health hazard

Objectives

After working through this chapter, you should be able to explain the following to friends and family:

- Appreciate the responsibilities of the person in charge
- Describe the seven principles of an HACCP plan
- Explain what active managerial control is

- Understand the necessity of a crisis management plan
- Describe the events that necessitate the closure of the operation
- Explain the steps necessary to re-open after a crisis-based closure

Recipe

Recipe: Chicken Alfredo with Broccoli

Chicken Alfredo is a widely popular meal, served in restaurants around the world. This recipe features the traditional American Alfredo sauce. The original Italian version does not contain heavy cream, making it a lighter, more buttery sauce, made with real Parmigiano Reggiano. With every meal we make, there is a level of safety and danger we have to observe and protect our food from. We will be using this recipe to highlight an HACCP plan (Hazard Analysis and Critical Control Points).

Ingredients:

- 400g (2 large) chicken legs, deboned
- 56g butter
- 1 clove garlic (minced)
- 237ml heavy cream
- 90g finely grated parmesan
- 227g penne pasta (or your favorite)
- 450g broccoli
- 60ml canola oil
- sea salt
- black pepper

Section 1

Reading assignment:

Read pages 259-265 in the coursebook, and then complete the activities below.

Fill in the missing words:

A safe and successful food operation will maintain a series of programs or _____
_____ designed to ensure that laws are followed, and that food is safe to
consume. Separating the totality of requirements into smaller manageable _____
can help focus training, re-training, and future material reference, which improves
staff retention and supports ___ _____ _____.

Questions:

Which of the following is not a food safety management program?

 a)   Personal hygiene program
 b)   Food safety program
 c)   Correct seasoning program
 d)   Clean-up of vomiting and diarrheal events program

What is the primary purpose of the PIC (Person in Charge)?

 a.   Operate the business in a profitable manner.
 b.   Open the doors on time and be present when closing.
 c.   Financial decisions and operational planning.
 d.   Maintain compliance with the Food Code.

A manager or person in charge must always maintain active managerial control over
the food establishment. This means what?

 a.   They understand the law.
 b.   They know the staff have been adequately trained.
 c.   They are prepared for an inspection at any time.
 d.   All of the above.

When an inspection occurs, problems that have already occurred are identified and
marked as what?

 a.   Legal Issuance
 b.   Violations
 c.   Root cause definitions
 d.   Categorical decision points

Individual Activity:

Students will create a Hazard Analysis and Critical Control Point report for the Chicken Alfredo recipe, using the seven points to ensure no vital areas are missed. With this dish, we will watch the video today, as it identifies everything we need to look for.

1.   Conduct a hazard analysis
2.   Determine the critical control points (CCPs)
3.   Establish critical limits
4.   Establish monitoring procedures
5.   Establish corrective actions
6.   Establish verification procedures
7.   Establish record-keeping and documentation procedures

After watching the Alfredo video begin by recording **HACCP step 1**, the hazard analysis, by identifying the following hazards that could occur:

Biological	Physical	Chemical

Section 2

Reading Assignment:
Read pages 266-279 in the coursebook, and then complete the activities below.

Fill in the missing words:
When the HACCP approach is embraced -- along with _____ _____, basic sanitation, and other prerequisite programs -- this _____ method assures _____ _____ control. The result is reduced risks and fewer violations during inspections.

Questions:
What does HACCP stand for?

    a.   Hazard Analysis and Critical Control points
    b.   Health Analysis and Critical Control Points
    c.   Hazard Analysis and Crucial Control Points
    d.   Health Analysis and Credible Control paths

When is a corrective action necessary in food production?

    a.   Any time a critical limit is not met.
    b.   All the time, to keep foods safe.
    c.   Only when chilling foods.
    d.   Only when cooking TCS foods.

A crisis management plan would be used when…

    a.   The owners of the restaurant feel it is necessary.
    b.   More than one danger has occurred in the restaurant.
    c.   Any time there are injuries in the restaurant.
    d.   There is an imminent health hazard.

A food operation must immediately discontinue operations and notify the regulatory authority if an imminent health hazard may exist. Which of the following does NOT count as one of these occurrences?

    a.   Power outage.
    b.   Water service interruption.
    c.   Telecommunications outage.
    d.   Sewage backup into the kitchen.

Individual Activity:

HACCP Step 2 — Using the chart, add the critical control points that occur during the storage, preparation and cooking processes. You may not need every single one (refrigeration, freezing, defrosting, cooking, hot holding etc.).

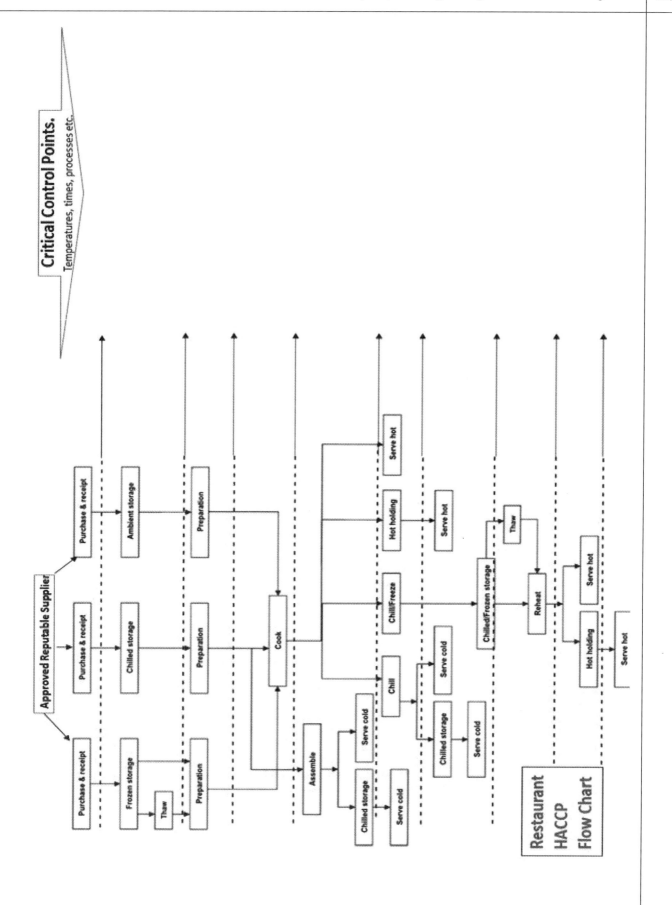

Section 3

Read the Chicken Alfredo recipe carefully and list all known Time & Temperature Control for Safety (TCS) ingredients.

Video Assignment:

Watch the Alfredo video again carefully and note any new skills needed.

Activity:

With your team, make a plan for what ingredients you can prepare for your mise en place. Make any needed or desired alterations to the recipe, as the vegetable and cut of chicken can be changed.

In the Kitchen:

- Measure & weigh the raw ingredients for your team's recipe. Depending on your available class time, your team may need to prepare some items. For instance, boning chicken thighs or fabricating whole chickens, depending on the instructor's preference and time.
- Wrap and label all ingredients and store them appropriately.
- Create and record your equipment mise en place list with your team to prepare for tomorrow's lab.

Individual Activity:

HACCP Step 3 —Look at the previous HACCP diagram to recall each level. What are the critical limits you will have to test for? (Example - minimum temperatures of foods, required dilutions of sanitizer etc.)

HACCP Step 4 —Look at the previous HACCP diagram to recall each level. What and how are you going to measure and record these Critical Control Points and how often? (Example – Chicken internal temperature to 165 Fahrenheit minimum with an insertion thermocouple.)

Section 4

Prepare the Chicken Alfredo & Broccoli with a team. Read the grading rubric to achieve the maximum points available.

In the Kitchen:

Each team checks their mise en place for the Chicken Alfredo (preparation of ingredients & equipment needed).

The team will follow the recipe. Create the Alfredo recipe with any assistance needed from the instructor or the preparation video.

Each team should wash, rinse, and sanitize their equipment and work surfaces to the standards shown in the video and discussed in the coursebook.

Record your results of success and compare with other teams making the Alfredo dish. Were there any variances between teams? What caused this?

Individual Activity

HACCP Step 5 —Look at the previous HACCP diagram to recall each level. Establish Corrective Actions that may need to occur. (Example - Food falls into the TDZ, reheat to 165 Fahrenheit. Sanitizer is too weak, add more to the correct limit.)

| |
| |
| |
| |
| |
| |
| |

Section 5

Individual Activity:

HACCP Step 6 —Establish Verification Procedures. Do the measurements occur? Are the corrective actions happening? How do we know training was completed? etc. Write below how these controls can be monitored to ensure a working HACCP plan.

| |
| |
| |
| |
| |
| |
| |

HACCP Step 7 —Establish record keeping & documentation procedures. Records can be used to verify the HACCP plan is working. Patterns might also be identified that reveal where additional staff training might be needed. When a foodborne illness outbreak occurs, these records can help authorities narrow down the problem to quickly contain the crisis. (Where do you record and what do you record?)

| |
| |
| |
| |
| |

Watch and participate in the end-of-chapter review video.

HACCP Plan Grading Rubric

Students will see examples of each section and professionally and accurately replicate the HACCP plan, arranging the sections in a logical easy to understand way and grouping them to maximize memory retention.

Students will be offered adequate time to complete the seven sections, with scrutiny on their written information, safety and sanitation, accuracy, attractiveness and the quality of their finished product.

It is recommended that students use simple examples to keep the information clear.

Safety and accuracy are key to your success.

Culinary Arts
HACCP Plan Rubric

Student name _____   Date _____

Category	Specifications	Highly Skilled (Professional) 25 pts	Skilled (First Cook) 20 pts	Moderately Skilled (Commis) 15pts	Low Skilled 10pts (Developing)	No Attempt 0pts	Comments
Written information 25pts	All written information is spelled correctly and is accurate	No guidance needed with all written information being accurate	Minimal guidance needed with all written information being accurate	Some guidance needed with all written information being accurate	Substantial guidance needed with all written information being accurate	No attempt made	
Safety & Sanitation 25pts	Correct information according to regulatory authority rules is presented	Exemplary standards maintained with no guidance	Very good standards maintained with some guidance	Good standards maintained, needed guidance	Poor standards maintained, needed guidance	No attempt made	
Accuracy of overall plan 25pts	Quality & precision of work, with accuracy of all 7 sections	Excellent precision with no guidance	Very good precision with some guidance	Good precision with guidance needed	Poor precision with guidance needed	No attempt made	
Quality of finished product 25pts	Final appearance of prepared HACCP Plan with quality work achieved	Excellent quality finished HACCP Plan, well presented	Very good quality finished plan, well presented	Good quality finished plan	Poor quality finished plan	No attempt made	

Chicken Alfredo Rubric

Students will see the video example, safely, professionally, and accurately replicating the Chicken Alfredo & Broccoli.

Students will be offered adequate time to complete this task, with scrutiny on their safety and sanitation, accuracy, attractiveness, and quality of their finished product.

Students should ensure all equipment and work surfaces are cleaned, sanitized and stored.

Safety and accuracy are key to your success.

Culinary Arts
Chicken Alfredo Recipe Rubric

Student name _____   Date _____

Category	Specifications	Highly Skilled (Professional) 25 pts	Skilled (First Cook) 20 pts	Moderately Skilled (Commis) 15pts	Low skilled 10pts (Developing)	No Attempt 0pts	Comments
Accuracy reading & following the recipe (25pts Max)	Reading, comprehending & following the recipe is done with accuracy	No guidance needed with reading, comprehending & following the recipe.	Minimal guidance needed with reading, comprehending & following the recipe.	Some guidance needed with reading, comprehending & following the recipe	Substantial guidance needed with reading, comprehending & following the recipe	No attempt made	
Safety & Sanitation (25pts Max)	Correctly following all regulatory authority rules when preparing foods.	Exemplary standards maintained with no guidance	Very good standards maintained with some guidance	good standards maintained, needed guidance	Poor standards maintained, needed guidance	No attempt made	
Accuracy & precision of preparations (25pts Max)	Accuracy & precision of work, with knife cuts & preparations.	Excellent precision with no guidance	Very good precision with some guidance	Good precision with guidance needed	Poor precision with guidance needed	No attempt made	
Quality of finished product (25pts Max)	Final appearance of prepared Chicken Alfredo with quality work achieved.	Excellent quality finished Chicken Alfredo, well presented.	Very good quality finished Chicken Alfredo, well presented.	Good quality finished Chicken Alfredo.	Poor quality finished product.	No attempt made	

Chapter Summary

The manager or person in charge is responsible for maintaining active managerial control of the food operation at all times. In addition to basic prerequisite programs such as personal hygiene and cleaning schedules, an HACCP plan can be used to identify, monitor, and verify major risk factors related to food safety. Doing so eliminates or maintains hazards at safe levels, where food is safe to consume.

Seven fundamental principles of an HACCP plan:

1. Conduct a hazard analysis
2. Determine the critical control points (CCPs)
3. Establish critical limits
4. Establish monitoring procedures
5. Establish corrective actions
6. Establish verification procedures
7. Establish record-keeping and documentation procedures

No one can predict when a disaster or emergent event will occur. Therefore, the management team should have a crisis management plan in place in order to respond quickly and keep food safe. Doing so will prevent foodborne illness, be a service to the community, and limit the loss of revenues due to food contamination.

Reasons to suspend operations:

- Fire
- Flood
- Extended interruption of:
    - Electrical service
    - Water service
    - Sewage backup
- Misuse of poisonous or toxic materials
- The onset of an apparent foodborne illness outbreak
- Gross insanitary occurrence or condition
- Other circumstances that may endanger public health

[Blank Page]

Chapter 14W

Regulations, Inspections, and Staff Training

A food safety manager has a lot of responsibilities, but some of the most important are covered in this chapter. It is not to say that staff training is more important than cooking chicken properly or preventing cross-contamination. However, if food handlers are not trained on the applicable rules (regulations) and what the rule enforcer (inspector) will look for, everything else will surely fail.

This chapter looks at the various governmental agencies involved in creating the Food Code and related regulations and how they are adopted and enforced in the United States. An interesting thing to be aware of is that the FDA Food Code is not a federal law, which means each jurisdiction (usually a state or tribal nation) has the authority to enact its own Food Code. Many choose to use the FDA Food Code or a slightly modified version. However, some have a unique version, making it critical to train even experienced staff as their experience may not be one hundred percent relevant.

Key Terms

Keep an eye out for these essential topics:

- Food and Drug Administration (FDA)
- FDA Food Code
- USDA Food Safety and Inspection Service (FSIS)
- Centers for Disease Control (CDC)
- Certified food protection manager
- Regulatory inspections
- Priority item
- Skills assessment

Objectives

After working through this chapter, you should be able to explain the following to friends and family:

- Describe the governmental entities involved in food
- Learn about the inspection process
- Explore how inspection violations must be handled

- Explain the general timeline of an inspection report
- Understand the benefits of staff training
- Describe the training methods

Recipe

Recipe: Fresh fruit displays, salads & parfait

Fruit displays, fruit salads, and parfaits are excellent snacks, and desserts that not only satiate that sweet tooth but also give valuable micronutrients. As a chef, we not only need to be able to prepare fruit for different purposes, but we must worry about how much wastage we get with it. Many fruits have inedible skins, seeds, pits, and cores. In this chapter, we will learn to understand how we manage the difference between the purchased amount (the whole fruit) and the edible portion that we call the yield.

Ingredients:

- 1 orange
- 1 pineapple
- 1 melon
- 1lb strawberries
- 6oz blueberries
- any other in-season available fruit you prefer
- 10oz vanilla or fruit Greek yogurt

Section 1

Reading assignment:

Read pages 283-292 in the main book, and then complete the activities below.

Fill in the missing words:

Governmental agencies involved in food safety are all funded by tax or tribal dollars with the directive to _____ the safety of food in the United States and tribal nations. However, the responsibility of _____ food from contamination must be shared between _____, regulating authorities, and consumers. Everyone must play a part in this critical public health initiative.

Questions:

What food products does the FDA (Food & Drug Administration) NOT have jurisdiction over the safety of?

- a) Some egg products, meats & poultry
- b) Eggs, Dairy & Shellfish
- c) Eggs, Meat & Shellfish
- d) Meats & Dairy

How many employees worked for the USDA in 2020?

- a. One hundred thousand
- b. One hundred & fifty thousand
- c. Two hundred & fifty thousand
- d. One million

Who has authority over food safety rules and regulations for food establishments in the US?

- a. USDA
- b. FDA
- c. State government
- d. OSHA

How are inspections of restaurants scheduled?

- a. Annually
- b. They are surprise visits
- c. Monthly
- d. They are booked a week in advance of the inspector's arrival

Individual Activity

If a chef needs 100 grams of pineapple per person for a party of 50 people, they can't purchase 5000 grams or 5 kilograms of pineapple. The problem the chef has to figure out is how much wastage they will have to deal with from the thick leathery skin, the core, and the spiky leaves that make up the crown. A good chef who controls their food cost will use culinary math to make sure they don't underestimate and upset customers and not overestimate and waste money.

Watch the culinary yield video, to see an explanation on how we can make this exercise easy to do and retain for the future.

Ingredient Yields

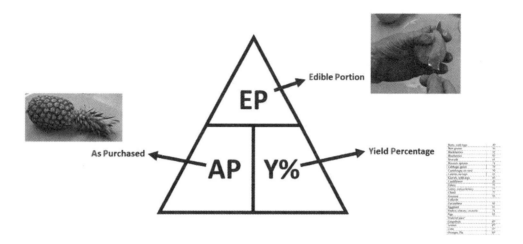

-We calculate the **Edible Portion (EP)** when we need to calculate what we will end up with for the customer to consume.

-The **As Purchased (AP)** is calculated to tell us what we need to buy, in order to end up with the right amount of finished product for what is needed.

-We can look up many standardized yields **(yield percentages Y%)** in books and online, but a chef can use this calculation to verify their staff is yielding the maximum viable product and not taking shortcuts and wasting commodities.

Ingredient Yields

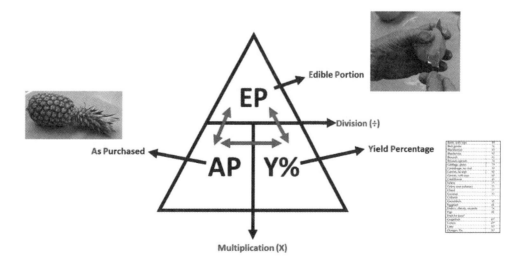

Whichever calculation you are making, use the other two in the triangle to get the answer. Remember if you are making a calculation vertically, you will need to divide. If you are making a calculation horizontally, then you will multiply.

Edible Portion (EP) = As Purchased (AP) X Yield Percentage (Y%)

As Purchased (AP) = Edible Portion (EP) ÷ Yield Percentage (Y%)

Yield Percentage (Y%)= Edible Portion (EP) ÷ As Purchased (AP)

Ingredient Yields

Fruit: Pineapple
Yield % = 52%
As purchased 2000g

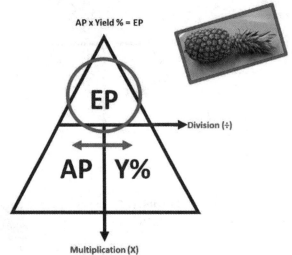

In this example, we will calculate the **(EP) Edible Portion** we will yield from the 2kg (2000g) **(AP) As Purchased** pineapple. We know from research that the typical **(YP) Yield Percentage** for this pineapple is 52%. Here is how we make the calculation:

AP   X Y% = EP

2000 X 52% = 1040g From my 2000g pineapple I could only serve 1040g of finished pineapple.

Section 2

Reading Assignment:

Read pages 293-295 in the main book, and then complete the activities below.

Fill in the missing words:

One of the most important jobs of a food manager is _____ _____. If staff does not understand the major food safety interventions, they can't possibly be expected to avoid them effectively. _____ _____ _____ training is the only way to have _____ _____ _____ and benefit from the preventive nature of an HACCP plan. When working with untrained or inexperienced staff, problems are bound to follow as the manager cannot be everywhere all at once.

Questions:

What are acceptable methods of assessing a new employee's food safety knowledge?

    a.   Verbally

    b.   Written

    c.   Software

    d.   All of the above

In order to have a quality food safety training program it needs to be:

    a.   Researched, created, and tested.

    b.   Developed, documented, and implemented.

    c.   Tried, tested, and targeted.

    d.   Brief, broad and biased.

Software-based training often uses a Learning Management System (LMS). What benefit is there to using this?

    a.   You can keep track of the employee's progress.

    b.   It's cheaper to operate.

    c.   It is quicker to eliminate possible bad staff members.

    d.   It's more fun for employees to use.

What is training by example?

    a.   Show an employee an example of what they should do, so they learn the process.

    b.   Teach employees what happens when they don't follow food safety rules. Make an example of them, generally by firing the employee.

    c.   Food safety managers should set an example for employees to mirror, by always setting a good example.

    d.   Show examples of training items on the notice boards in the break room.

Individual Activity:

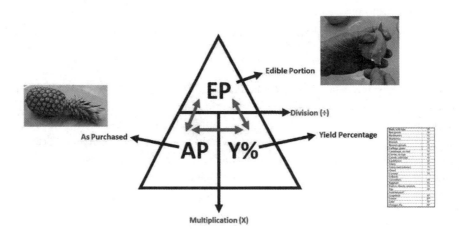

Here is a reminder of the calculations and the chart we use to visualize solving the equations.

Edible Portion (EP) = As Purchased (AP) X Yield Percentage (Y%)

As Purchased (AP) = Edible Portion (EP) ÷ Yield Percentage (Y%)

Yield Percentage (Y%) = Edible Portion (EP) ÷ As Purchased (AP)

Solve the following using the knowledge you have gained:

Janice has a party of 50 who will have strawberries for dessert. Each person will have 150g each, making a total need of 7500g of finished edible sliced strawberries. With a yield percentage of 89%, how much does Janice need to purchase?

If there is time in this class, your instructor can give you additional equations to calculate.

Section 3

Read the Fresh fruit Displays, salads & parfait recipe carefully and list all known Time & Temperature Control for Safety (TCS) ingredients.

Video Assignment:

Watch the fruit preparation video carefully and note any new skills needed.

Activity:

With your team, make a plan for what ingredients your team will prepare. Make any needed alterations due to the seasonal availability of products.

In the Kitchen:

- Measure & weigh the raw ingredients for your team's recipe. Don't wash the fruits in advance, as they can start to deteriorate when they are stored wet. They will be washed before preparation tomorrow.

- Wrap and label all ingredients and store them appropriately.

- Create and record your equipment mise en place list with your team to be ready for tomorrow's practical.

Individual Activity

Ingredient Yields

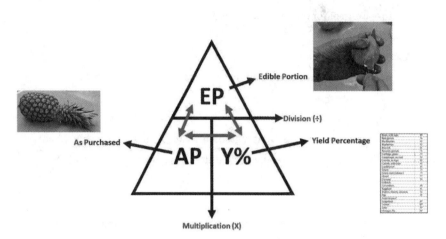

Edible Portion (EP)   = As Purchased (AP) X Yield Percentage (Y%)

As Purchased (AP)   = Edible Portion (EP) ÷ Yield Percentage (Y%)

Yield Percentage (Y%)= Edible Portion (EP) ÷ As Purchased (AP)

Solve the following using the knowledge you have gained:

1)   George thinks some of his apprentice chefs are taking short cuts and wasting too much of his product, as they prepare fruit. He chooses to do a spot check on the pineapples. They prepared 10kg (10,000g) of whole **as purchased pineapples** and ended with 4500g (4.5kg) of finished Edible Portion (EP) that was served to customers. What was their **Yield Percentage (Y%)?**

2)   Sonya has a small case of cantaloupe melons. They total to 5750g (5.75kg) **As Purchased (AP).** She needs to have 2800g (2.8kg) **Edible Portion (EP) for her display.** The **Yield Percentage (Y%)** for Cantaloupe is 50%. Does she have enough melon?

If there is time in this class, your instructor can give you additional equations to calculate.

Section 4

Prepare the fruit display with your team. Read the grading rubric, to achieve the maximum points available. You will also take all measurements in the chart for each type of fruit you prepare, to use your culinary yield skills.

In the Kitchen:

Each team creates its mise en place for the display only. Save some fruit for a fruit salad and parfait tomorrow but measure all the weights for all the fruit below (preparation of ingredients & equipment needed).

The team will follow the recipe. Create the display with any assistance needed from the instructor or the preparation video. Follow all steps in the preparation to successfully create an attractive display.

Wash, rinse & sanitize all equipment and tables used, completing this as a team.

Fruit measured	As purchased weight	Waste	Edible Portion	

Section 5

Team Activity

Prepare the fruit salad and fruit parfait with your team. Use your imagination and make your dishes look attractive. Blending fruit with the yogurt can create different colors and layers. Keep the flavors simple, to ensure balance. Read the grading rubric, to achieve the maximum points available.

Wash, rinse & sanitize all equipment and tables used, completing this as a team.

Each team should present their works and compare the different displays created. Taste the different parfaits and take note how variances in fruit choices can influence the outcome.

Note below what you would do differently next time to change or enhance the recipe:

_____

_____

_____

_____

-In **Section 4** there was an additional column that was not yet used. This is where you need to calculate the achieved **yield percentage** for each fruit you prepared. Remember to use the equation for calculating **Yield Percentage (YP)**

Watch and participate in the end-of-chapter review video.

_____

_____

_____

_____

_____

_____

_____

_____

_____

_____

_____

_____

_____

Grading Rubric- Yield Math

Students will use their knowledge and skills to precisely conduct an investigation into the methods we use to calculate the "As purchased" "Edible Portion" and "Yield percentage" we find with fruit.

Students will be offered adequate time to complete this task, with scrutiny of their written information, safety and sanitation knowledge, accuracy, attractiveness, and the quality of their finished document.

Safety and accuracy are key to your success.

Culinary Arts
Yield Math Rubric

Student name _____   Date _____

Category	Specifications	Highly Skilled (Professional) 25 pts	Skilled (First Cook) 20 pts	Moderately Skilled (Commis) 15pts	Low Skilled 10pts (Developing)	No Attempt 0pts	Comments
Written information 25pts	All written information is spelled correctly and is accurate	No guidance needed with all written information being accurate	Minimal guidance needed with all written information being accurate	Some guidance needed with all written information being accurate	Substantial guidance needed with all written information being accurate	No attempt made	
Show your calculations 25pts	Correct information showing your work	Exemplary standards shown with no guidance	Very good standards maintained with some guidance	Good standards maintained, needed guidance	Poor standards maintained, needed guidance	No attempt made	
Accuracy of overall yield math 25pts	Quality & precision of work, with accuracy of yield math	Excellent precision with no guidance	Very good precision with some guidance	Good precision with guidance needed	Poor precision with guidance needed	No attempt made	
Quality of finished presentation 25pts	Final appearance of prepared presentation with quality work achieved	Excellent quality finished presentation, well presented	Very good quality finished presentation well presented	Good quality finished presentation	Poor quality finished presentation	No attempt made	

Grading Rubric- Fresh Fruit Displays, Salad & Parfaits

Students will see the video example, safely, professionally, and accurately replicating the fruit items.

Students will be offered adequate time to complete this task, with scrutiny on their safety and sanitation, accuracy, attractiveness, and quality of their finished product.

Students should ensure all equipment and work surfaces are cleaned, sanitized, and stored.

Safety and accuracy are key to your success.

Culinary Arts
Fruit Platter Recipe Rubric

Student name _____   Date _____

Category	Specifications	Highly Skilled (Professional) 25 pts	Skilled (First Cook) 20 pts	Moderately Skilled (Commis) 15pts	Low skilled 10pts (Developing)	No Attempt 0pts	Comments
Accuracy reading & following the recipe (25pts Max)	Reading, comprehending & following the recipe is done with accuracy	No guidance needed with reading, comprehending & following the recipe.	Minimal guidance needed with reading, comprehending & following the recipe.	Some guidance needed with reading, comprehending & following the recipe	Substantial guidance needed with reading, comprehending & following the recipe	No attempt made	
Safety & Sanitation (25pts Max)	Correctly following all regulatory authority rules when preparing foods.	Exemplary standards maintained with no guidance	Very good standards maintained with some guidance	good standards maintained, needed guidance	Poor standards maintained, needed guidance	No attempt made	
Accuracy & precision of preparations (25pts Max)	Accuracy & precision of work, with knife cuts & preparations.	Excellent precision with no guidance	Very good precision with some guidance	Good precision with guidance needed	Poor precision with guidance needed	No attempt made	
Quality of finished product (25pts Max)	Final appearance of prepared Fruit Platter with quality work achieved.	Excellent quality finished fruit platter, well presented.	Very good quality finished fruit platter, well presented.	Good quality finished fruit platter.	Poor quality finished product.	No attempt made	

Chapter Summary

The food safety manager must be able to demonstrate their knowledge during an inspection. To do this, they must be trained, understand the applicable rules, and be cooperative with an inspector. The inspector will also ask staff questions about what they are doing, so staff also need to be trained.

Staff training is a critical mechanism that ties everything necessary about food safety together. When adequately developed and implemented, a staff training program will be the solid foundation for a successful business for many years!

Timeframe for Food Code violation corrections:

- Priority Item   72 hours
- Priority Foundation Item   10 calendar days
- HACCP plan deviation   10 calendar days
- Core Item   90 calendar days

[Blank Page]

Chapter 15W
Practice Exam

This chapter will highlight the practice exam software provided with this book, including accessing the exam, installing, required files, user interface and how to interpret the results. Taking this practice exam, after studying this book and accompanying student workbook, will help ensure a successful result when taking the actual ServSafe Manager Certification exam, either in a classroom or a proctored online exam.

The practice exam questions are similar, not identical, to the actual exam.

Important Things to Know
Here are a few big picture things you should keep in mind:

- **Practice Exam – First Steps**
    - The practice exam, that comes with this book, is taken on **your own computer**
    - You must download the practice exam software from SDC Publications
        - See inside-front cover of this book for access instructions
    - Note which questions you got wrong, and study those topics

- **Practice Exam - Details**
    - Questions: 90
    - Timed: 90 minutes
    - Passing: 70%
    - Results: Presented upon completion

The practice exam can be taken multiple times. There are over 300 questions total, which are shuffled each time the exam is taken, making each attempt unique. Although the questions are shuffled, there is still a balanced number per chapter.

This practice exam can be taken multiple times.

Practice Exam Overview

The **practice exam** included with this book can be downloaded from the publisher's website using the **access code** found on the inside-front cover. This is a good way to check your skills prior to taking the official exam, as the intent is to offer similar questions in roughly the same format as the formal exam. This practice exam is taken at home, work, or school, on your own computer.

This is a test drive for the exam process, including:

- Understanding the exam software
- Exam question format
- Managing time
- How the results are presented at the exam conclusion

Here is a sample of what the practice exam looks like...

Sample question from included practice exam

Having taken the practice exam can remove some anxiety one may have going into an exam that may positively impact a career search or advancement in school.

Download and Install the Practice Exam

Follow the instructions on the inside-front cover of this book, using the provided access code to download the practice exam. Once the ZIP file is downloaded you must extract the files into a folder that you create.

Suggested steps:

- Create a folder on your desktop or C drive, such as **C:\ServSafe Manager Certification Practice Exam**
- Double-click on the downloaded ZIP file
- Copy all the folders/files from the ZIP file to the newly created folder

The image below shows the files copied to the recommended folder. Note that the practice exam cannot run from within the downloaded Zip file.

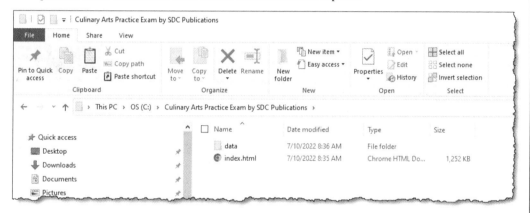

Practice exam files saved to a folder

Starting the Exam

To start the practice exam, double-click on the **index.html** file pointed out in the previous image (step #2). Once started, you will see the screen shown next. This practice exam software runs in your internet browser. Click the blue **Start Quiz** button to begin the practice exam.

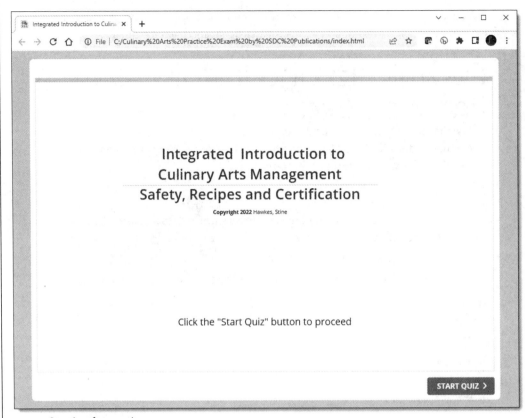

Starting the practice exam

If you enter your name and email address at the beginning of the practice exam, you will receive an email with your result. If you are required to take the practice exam for a class, the 'results email' can then be forwarded to your instructor. Alternatively, you could also enter your instructor's email address. Whether you enter your name and email address or not, neither the author nor SDC Publications captures any data related to this practice exam.

No exam data is collected by the author or publisher of this book.

This step is optional. Simply leave the fields blank and click Submit to proceed without entering your name or email address.

Enter Your Details (optional)

> Name

> Email

Results will be sent to this email

Privacy Statement:
This information is only used to email the result to you, or whatever email address you enter. Leave these blank to skip sending results altogether.

Copyright 2022 Hawkes, Stine

SUBMIT

Enter name and email address to recieve results (optional step)

Practice Exam User Interface (UI)

The following image, and subsequent list, highlight the features of the practice exam's user interface.

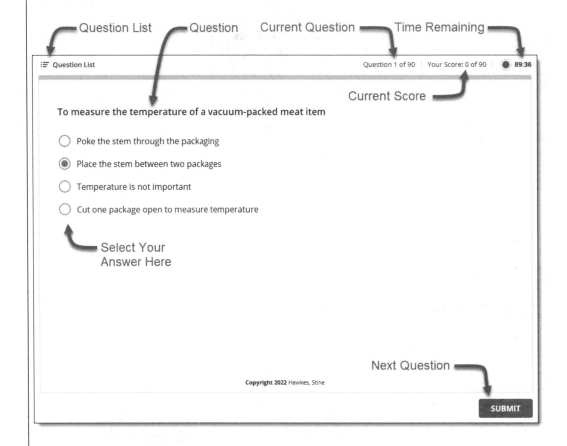

User Interface details:

- **Question List:** Opens a menu listing all questions
- **Question:** Practice exam question
- **Enter Your Answer Here:** Select an answer
- **Current Question:** Current number out of 90
- **Current Score:** Each correct answer is worth 1 point, 90 total points possible
- **Time Remaining:** Time remaining for the 90-minute timed exam
- **Next Question:** Click Submit to proceed to the next question

Practice Exam Results

When you complete the practice exam, you immediately find out if you passed or failed. Be sure to click the **Detailed Report** and **Review Quiz** options and note which questions were answered incorrectly and review those related sections in the book.

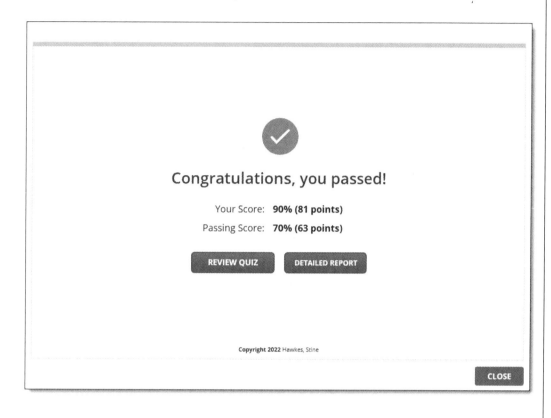

Notice, in the Detailed Report shown in the next image, the results are grouped by chapters in the book. Use this information to know which chapters to go back and review, if needed.

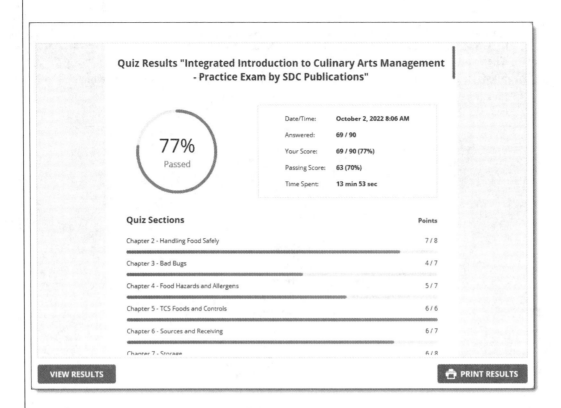

While reviewing the results, a green check mark will appear next to the correct answer. Clicking the **Questions List** button in the upper left will provide an overview list of all questions as shown in the next image.

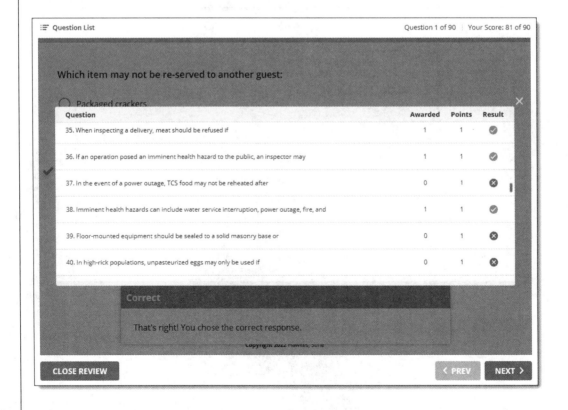

Conclusion

As with any formal exam, the more you practice the more likely you are to have successful results. So, be sure to take the time to download the provided practice exam and give it a try before you sit for the actual exam.

Good luck!

[Blank Page]

Chapter 16W
Certification Study Guide

This chapter can be used to study for an in-class quiz or the official certification exam. It is impossible to cover everything that might be on the exam, even in the entire coursebook, as the authors do not know the questions. The official exam is based on the current version of the FDA Food Code.

Food Safety Basics

Following these basic guidelines will ensure that food is free from contaminants or is held to safe levels to prevent foodborne illness.

Food should be:

- Heated or cooled to specific temperatures
- Not be left out for extended periods
- Covered and stored properly
- Stored separately from chemicals and cleaners

Foodborne Illnesses

Over 40 different kinds of bacteria, viruses, parasites, and molds that may occur in food can cause foodborne illness. A foodborne illness is commonly referred to as food poisoning or stomach flu.

These include illnesses such as E. coli and Listeriosis (infection from Listeria exposure). Ensuring foods remain free from foodborne illnesses can be achieved in two ways: through proper storage and proper cooking. Proper storage requires that food handlers store all food in temperatures **below 41°F** (41° C) **for refrigeration and exceeding 135°F** (57° C) **for storing hot holding and cooking**. Foods held between these temperatures should only be given a 4-hour window before they are either placed back into storage or thrown away. Foods being cooked should first be cooked to **135°F** (57° C) **and higher** to kill any remaining germs.

Foods must be cooked to the minimum internal cooking temperature and stored accordingly when refrigerated:

Storage order in refrigerator (top to bottom)	Minimum internal cooking temperature
Ready to Eat food (RTE) (ham, cheese, tomatoes, cucumber etc.)	N/A
Seafood (shell fish, fin fish etc.)	**145° Fahrenheit** (63° C)
Whole Cuts of Beef, Veal, Lamb & Pork (Intact meat) (steaks & chops etc.)	**145° Fahrenheit** (63° C)
Ground Meats & Ground Fish (Nonintact Meat) (burgers, fish mousse, pasta sauce etc.)	**155° Fahrenheit** (68° C)
Whole & Ground Poultry (chicken, turkey etc.)	**165° Fahrenheit** (74° C)

While most foodborne illnesses result from bacterial contamination, some illnesses have been caused by viruses and diseases from food service workers. For this reason, it is vitally important to wear protective gear when handling food (keeping hair away from food and avoiding skin-to-food contact) and to practice proper hygiene by washing your hands for a minimum of 10-15 seconds with warm water and soap.

While foodborne illnesses pose a risk to everyone, specific populations are more at risk than others. They are:

- Preschool-age children
- The elderly
- People who are immunocompromised

Biological, Physical, and Chemical Contaminants

Food contamination takes on many forms, including biological, physical, and chemical forces and potential allergens. Contamination can occur due to improper food storage (storing food next to chemicals), improper growing conditions, exposure to parasites, and incorrect use of preparation materials. Below, each of these will be tackled and identified.

Biological Contaminants

Biological contaminants are contaminants found in nature. These include bacteria, parasites, fungi, and environmental toxins. The best way to prevent contamination from biological agents is to adhere to food storage and preparation guidelines, keeping foods at the proper temperatures during storage and cooking.

- **Bacteria:** Bacteria thrive in moist environments between 41°F and 135°F. They are most active from 70-120°F. The FDA considers three types of bacteria as most dangerous because they are very contagious and cause severe illness: Salmonella Typhi, Shigella, and Escherichia Coli, more commonly referred to as E.coli.

- **Salmonella:** Salmonella comes from people and is often found in beverages or ready-to-eat foods such as fruits and vegetables. The best way to prevent salmonella is to wash your hands and ensure all food is cooked to the proper temperature.

- **Shigella:** Shigella originates from human feces. It is spread from flies and improper hand-washing. The best way to prevent Shigella is to observe good hygiene practices and eliminate insects around food.

- **E. coli:** E. coli originates from cattle intestines and is found in ground beef or fresh produce that may be contaminated from farm runoff, such as lettuce or strawberries. The best way to avoid E. coli is to avoid cross-contamination between ground beef and other foods and to always wash produce before ingestion.

- **Viruses:** Viruses do not grow in food but can be transferred to food through the fecal-oral route. Sneezing, coughing, and improper hand-washing practices are some of the most common routes of transmission. Hepatitis A and the Norovirus are the most common viruses found in food. They are typically linked with ready-to-eat foods and shellfish.

- **Parasites:** Parasites are most often found in seafood, wild game meats, and foods that have been washed with contaminated water. To eliminate parasites, always cook foods to the recommended temperature. If the seafood or meat is supposed to be served undercooked or raw (such as in sushi or sashimi), ensure it is stored at the proper temperature and served to the guest immediately.

- **Fungi:** Fungi includes yeasts, molds, and mushrooms. Fungi pose a problem when they produce toxins that can make the consumer sick. Always be sure the mushrooms you are serving are safe to eat, and throw out any food that has developed mold. In addition to the typical vomiting/diarrhea that many foodborne illnesses cause, ingesting toxic fungi can also cause neurological symptoms, such as a reverse hot/cold sensation or tingling in the extremities.

Physical Contaminants

Physical contaminants refer to contaminants of an actual foreign physical object. These can include insects or other foreign pests in food or may refer to shards of broken metal or other small, potentially hazardous objects that may be found in food. This also includes human items such as fingernails, hair, and skin. The best means of avoiding this particular contaminant is through a thorough inspection of food items and observation of safe food preparation and hygiene guidelines.

Chemical Contaminants

Chemical contaminants are contaminants from cleaning supplies, improper surface materials, improper metals, and pesticides. While some pesticide exposure cannot be avoided in conventional foods, thorough cleaning of pesticide-exposed food greatly lessens the chemical contaminant. To avoid chemical contamination in other mediums, store and use cleaning materials a great distance from all food items, and wait the recommended time before using a surface cleaned with chemical agents. Adhere to the rules of food preparation and avoid using soft or unsafe metals and plastics in cooking.

Allergens

While allergens are not unsafe for everyone, even the slightest amount of exposure to a food allergy can prove toxic. For this reason, you must acquaint yourself with the equipment you use, the manufacturing facilities your food employs, and the ingredients found in your food items. To avoid allergen exposure during food preparation, be sure to clean and sanitize surfaces and utensils before and after each use. Acquaint yourself and your employees with common food allergies, and be aware of the presence of these allergens in your food. Train employees in the signs of allergic responses too.

The BIG 9 common allergies include nuts, peanuts, dairy, soy, shellfish, eggs, fish, wheat & sesame.

The Flow of Food

As food comes in and out of your establishment, it requires safe handling and preparation. While it may seem simple enough to receive and store food, you must ensure that all received food is stored properly and is within its safe use dates. As food enters and leaves an establishment, it must constantly be monitored for freshness and safety.

Purchasing, Receiving, and Storing

When purchasing food, always be sure to purchase from **approved reputable suppliers**. While it may be tempting to ship food in from unapproved areas, or to go for the cheapest food option, adhering to safety guidelines while producing and storing food is pivotal. Read company statements and practices before deciding to purchase with that particular entity, and make sure safe practices are being followed.

When food is being received, it must adhere to all federal and state guidelines. In addition, you must ensure that all food is delivered at safe temperatures. Here are some guidelines to keep in mind:

- 41°F or colder for cold foods
- 45°F or lower for **live** shellfish, milk, and eggs (then cool rapidly to 41°F and below)
- 135°F or hotter for hot food
- All frozen foods must remain frozen during delivery 0°F and below.

No matter which type of food you are handling, it should always be promptly stored after being received. Proper food storage: cold foods should be stored at 41°F or lower, while hot foods must be stored at 135°F or higher. Failure to do so will likely result in the introduction of foodborne illness due to bacterial contamination.

Preparation

As mentioned above, proper food preparation is essential in delivering safe, high quality food. When preparing food, be sure to use only high-quality (NSF certified) metal and plastic utensils, and be sure to properly clean and sanitize all preparation surfaces and utensils. When cooking, vegetables and fruits should be cooked to 135°F or higher; fish, steaks and pork chops to 145; ground meats to 155 and poultry should be cooked to 165°F or higher.

Before cooking, food should be thawed via a refrigerator (most preferable for quality & safety), cool running water, a microwave or as part of the cooking process.

Cooling

Cooling foods should be completed as quickly as possible, to limit pathogen growth and maintain food quality. Once foods reach 135 Fahrenheit they must be cooled to 70

Fahrenheit within 2 hours. If this is not successfully done, the food must be reheated to 165 and cooling reattempted. Once at 70 Fahrenheit a further maximum of 4 hours is permitted to reach 41 Fahrenheit or below. This can be completed using ice as an ingredient, blast chiller, ice and water bath, ice paddle, spreading foods across a wider area, among other things. Make sure to consider the container material, as conductive materials such as metals will cool faster than insulating plastics. Food above 70°F should never be placed in a refrigerator, otherwise damage can occur to the refrigerator, considerable condensation build up can occur and possible contamination to other foods too.

Serving

When serving food, be keenly aware of all food temperatures. Food should not be allowed to remain between 41°F and 135°F for too long. **Cold food not refrigerated cannot be allowed to rise above 70 Fahrenheit and must be discarded after no more than 6 hours. Hot food cannot be left out more than 4 hours**; food left out for more than 4 hours must be discarded. Serving already-served food is not permitted unless food is sealed and untouched (ketchup packets, sealed crackers etc.). Finally, self-service stations (buffets) should only be used with fresh plates. **Patrons should not be permitted to reuse dirty plates** or utensils because this can contaminate dishes placed out for service.

Food Safety Management Systems

Before employees are permitted to work with food, safety programs should have taken place instructing the proper implementation of personal hygiene, food service and preparation, and managerial practices. Managerial practices include constantly checking food stations and workers to ensure the necessary practices are being observed. Management should also never admit fault in the case of a foodborne illness outbreak. Instead, management should work to discover the initial culprit and immediately eradicate said cause.

Cleaning and Sanitation

Cleaning and sanitation are extremely important in maintaining a well-rounded, safe eating environment. Proper cleaning will help eradicate pests such as mice and cockroaches, while sanitation will assist in warding off foodborne illness and cross-contamination between food items. Following the procedures for cleaning and sanitizing will ensure both workers and customers enjoy a hassle-free, safe dining experience.

Principles of Cleaning and Sanitation

Cleaning and sanitizing are different actions but generally go hand in hand. Cleaning is the process of removing food or other items from a surface; sanitizing is the act of removing organisms from a surface to improve safety and reduce the risk of exposure to harmful bacteria, viruses or fungi. The two come together in a compound process: wash, rinse, sanitize, and air dry. Failure to complete these steps in that order will result in an ineffective washing and sanitizing process. Both cleaning and sanitizing agents should be stored well away from food items, and rags and other cleaning tools should be changed at least every 4 hours to prevent contamination.

Always follow the instructions for chemical dilution, to ensure safety & efficacy.

- Chlorine (Bleach) concentration: 50 to 100 ppm.

- Quaternary Ammonia (QUAT, QAC) concentration: Per manufacturer's instruction, but often 200ppm.

- Iodine concentration: 12.5 to 25 ppm.

Pest Management

Pest management involves three steps: **denying pets access** to the establishment; **deny pests food, shelter, and water**; and work with a **licensed pest control operator** to remove any pests that have made a home for themselves. While prevention is best, be on the lookout for signs of any existing pest issues. These include roach droppings and egg casings (pepper-like spots and cases that look like thick grains of dark rice), and rodent droppings and actions (including gnawing, nesting, and leaving tracks). Just as cleaning agents should be stored away from food, on-site pest removal agents must be stored away from food. Professional pest removal should be completed after business hours and after employees have gone home, and all surfaces should be cleaned and sanitized thoroughly before use.

[Blank Page]

Chapter 17W
Glossary

Abrasive Cleaner is a strong cleaner, sometimes with a gritty texture, to penetrate and loosen heavily soiled surfaces such as food baked onto a pan. Care must be used as some surfaces, like non-stick pans, may be scratched.

Accredited Program describes a food protection manager certification program that has been evaluated and listed by an accrediting agency. It does not refer to training functions or educational programs.

Acid Cleaner with a pH below 7.0, is used on mineral deposits and oxidation on surfaces that alkaline cleaners can't remove, such as rust, scale, and tarnish. These cleaners cannot come in contact with skin or eyes and may damage surfaces if not used properly.

Acidity is a measure of the level of acid in food. Slightly acidic food with a pH ranging from 4.6 to 7.5 is called potentially hazardous food. Galvanized metal or copper surfaces should not come in contact with acidic food as dangerous contaminants, in the form of toxins, may be transferred to the food. Food examples with a pH 4 or less: soda, grains, sugar, and alcohol.

Active Managerial Control describes an operation's responsibility for proactively developing and implementing food safety management systems to prevent, eliminate, or reduce the occurrence of foodborne illness risk factors. Through the use of HACCP principles, active managerial control is achieved by identifying the food safety hazards attributed to products, determining the necessary steps to control the identified risks, and implementing ongoing practices or procedures to ensure safe food.

Additive, Food is any substance that results in it becoming a component or otherwise affecting the characteristic of any food.

Additive, Color means a dye, pigment, or other substance, which is capable of imparting color when added or applied to a food and required premarket approval.

Adulterated describes food that bears or contains any poisonous substance which may render it injurious to health. Economically motivated adulterated means food is considered adulterated if misbranded or a valuable ingredient of the food is left out or taken out, or ingredients are added to increase the product weight.

Approved means acceptable based on a determination of conformity with principles, practices, and generally recognized standards that protect public health according to the regulating authority.

Air Curtain is a device that blows a consistent stream of air across a door opening, creating an air barrier, which limits the entrance of contaminants and flying insects. Energy can also be saved by limiting the amount of conditioned air that leaves the building every time the door is opened.

Air Gap is an air space with no physical connection (permanent or temporary) between a potable water supply outlet and another water source. For example, the tip of a faucet should never come in contact with the water in a full sink compartment (a temporary physical connection). The only reliable method for preventing backflow is an air gap.

Ambient Temperature/ Air Temperature is a measure of air temperature immediately surrounding food, but not the surface or food itself.

ALERT is a mnemonic device for the FDA's food defense program, which stands for assure, look, employees, reports, and threat.

Alkalinity is a measure of the level of alkali in food. Examples of low-acidic foods with a pH of 7.0 or higher are soy, most vegetables, and most fruits. Most types of food are not alkaline.

Allergen is a substance, often a protein, that causes an allergic response that can be severe or fatal to some. Examples include pollen, molds, and certain foods.

Americans with Disabilities Act (ADA) is a U.S. civil rights law enacted in 1990 that prohibits discrimination against individuals with disabilities in all areas of public life.

Amnesic Shellfish Poisoning (ASP) is a potentially deadly illness caused by ingesting shellfish that have eaten toxic algae. This toxin, called domoic acid, cannot be destroyed through freezing or cooking. Shellfish like clams, mussels, oysters, and scallops must be purchased through approved and reputable vendors.

Anaphylaxis is an allergic reaction to an allergen that can be severe or fatal to some.

Anisakis simplex is a human parasite infestation caused by the ingestion of larvae of several species of ascaridoid nematodes (roundworms), which are sometimes called "herringworm", "codworm", or "sealworm", in undercooked marine fish. Fish should be cooked to the minimum internal temperature, or, if served raw, sushi-grade fish should be purchased through approved and reputable vendors to avoid illness.

Approved Suppliers are suppliers who follow federal, state, local, or tribal food handling, packaging, and delivery standards. They become approved by reputation and consistent service, including timely deliveries, and properly packaged products that arrive at the correct temperatures to avoid time-temperature abuse. Buying from an unapproved, or untested, supplier puts an operation at risk, which can lead to foodborne illness and tarnish an operation's reputation.

Aseptically Packaged is a process by which microorganisms are prevented from entering a package during and after packaging. During aseptic processing, a sterilized package is filled with a commercially sterile food product and sealed within the confines of a hygienic environment.

Asymptomatic describes an individual infected with a pathogen but not exhibiting or producing any signs or symptoms of vomiting, diarrhea, or jaundice. Second definition: symptoms of an infected person have subsided and they are now considered to be asymptomatic.

Bacillus Cereus (B. cereus) is a spore-forming bacterium that produces toxins that cause vomiting or diarrhea. Symptoms are generally mild and short-lived (up to 24 hours). B. cereus is commonly found in the environment (e.g. soil) as well as in a variety of foods (e.g. cooked potatoes, corn, and rice). Spores can survive harsh environments including normal cooking temperatures.

Backflow happens when potable water flows opposite to its intended direction, either from a loss of pressure in the supply lines (public side) or an increase in pressure in an establishment (private side). In either case, if any affected food establishment's pipes include a cross-connection, contaminants could be drawn through the cross-connection into that establishment's pipes—and, if the backflow continues, perhaps even into the public water mains.

Bacteria is a common foodborne contaminant made up of a single cell. Most bacteria are not harmful, but some can cause illness when they are ingested, usually with food. Another source of foodborne illness is toxins produced by bacteria.

Bacterial Growth describes the number, not size, of bacteria as they grow by splitting into two cells. The mnemonic device FAT TOM describes environmental conditions affecting the growth rate of bacteria. There are four phases of bacterial growth: slow growth (lag-phase), rapid growth (log-phase), equilibrium (stationary phase), and reduction (death phase).

Balut is an embryo inside a fertile egg that has been incubated for a period sufficient for the embryo to reach a specific stage of development after which it is removed from incubation before hatching.

Best-by date is the month, day, and year a product should be consumed by for best quality and taste according to the manufacturer.

Beverage is a liquid for drinking, including water.

Bimetallic Stemmed Thermometer is a standard thermometer used to measure the internal temperature of food. They have a range of 0° F to 220° F (-18° C to 104° C) and have a wide range of uses, from receiving to cooking to monitoring hot or cold food items. The sensing area extends from the tip of the metal stem up to the dimple.

Biological Contaminant describes pathogenic-type contaminants, such as viruses, bacteria, parasites, fungi, and toxins, which can lead to foodborne illness. Some toxins are a byproduct of bacteria while others occur naturally in some fish, plants, and mushrooms.

Blast Chiller is a specialized unit designed to quickly lower the temperature of food by approximately 100° F (38° C) in 90 seconds. The primary goal is to quickly move a food's temperature through the time-temperature danger zone to prevent bacteria growth. Using a blast chiller immediately after food preparation helps ensure it is safe for consumption later when properly stored.

Bodily Fluids are liquids found within the human body, such as blood, saliva, urine, feces, perspiration, pus from a wound, and oily secretions produced by the skin and hair. Pathogens in these bodily fluids can contaminate food and cause foodborne illness if not properly contained.

Boiling-point Method is used to calibrate a thermometer, that varies by altitude. When inserted into boiling water, the thermometer should be adjusted to read 212° F (100° C) at sea level.

Bottled Drinking Water is water contained in sealed unopened bottles, packages, or other containers and offered for sale for human consumption, including bottled mineral water.

Botulism is a severe foodborne illness caused by toxins produced by Clostridium botulinum bacteria. Emergency medical care is required, including breathing assistance and antitoxins.

Calibration is a thermometer adjustment to ensure proper alignment to a known standard, such as the water's boiling point or freezing point. Note that the boiling point of water varies by altitude. Thermometers should be calibrated before use, after storage, if dropped, and between a large temperature range.

Campylobacter jejuni is a leading cause of bacterial foodborne illness commonly associated with undercooked poultry. Preventative measures include cooking to the minimum internal temperature and avoiding cross-contamination.

Cantilever-mounted is a wall-mounted work surface or equipment designed to enhance the ability to clean around it, including the floor below.

Carrier is a term used to describe a host for a pathogenic microorganism, such as a human, animal, or insect. A carrier may be asymptomatic and infect others directly or through contaminated food. Carriers are excluded from working in food establishments to protect the public.

Casing is a tubular container for sausage products made of either natural or artificial (synthetic) material.

Catering is a food and beverage service offered remotely at a location selected by the customer. Catering is a service some restaurants offer but can also be the only service some businesses provide. Requires special vehicles and equipment to transport food, serve at the correct temperatures, and keep food out of the time-temperature danger zone.

Celsius is an international scale of temperature where 0° C is aligned with the freezing point of water and 100° C, at sea level, with the boiling point of water.

Centers for Disease Control and Prevention (CDC) is the national health agency under the U.S. Department of Health and Human Services. They investigate and provide health-related reports about foodborne illness outbreaks and how to prevent them.

Ceramic Tile is a hard-wearing ceramic or stone material set in grout and installed on floors and walls, especially in wet or food production areas.

Certification Number means the unique identification number issued by the shellfish control authority to each dealer for each location. Each certification number shall consist of a one-to-five digit Arabic number preceded by the two letter state abbreviation and followed by a two-letter abbreviation for the type of activity or activities the dealer is qualified to perform in accordance with this provision of the National Shellfish Sanitation Program using the terms in the following tables:

Table A. Certifications

ACRONYM	TERM
SP	Shucker Packer
RP	Repacker
SS	SHELLSTOCK Shipper
RS	Reshipper
DP	Depuration

Table B. Permits

ACRONYM	TERM
PHP	Post-Harvest Processing
AQ	Aquaculture
WS	Wet Storage

Chemical Agent is a substance found in many cleaning, sanitizing, lubricating, and pesticide products used within a foodservice organization. These products are often hazardous but are required to accomplish specific tasks, so they must be stored and used correctly.

Chemical Bait is a substance designed to destroy harmful pests, such as insects or rodents, within a foodservice establishment to help prevent foodborne illnesses from contaminated food. The bait is contained within an enclosed container with holes only large enough for the pest to enter, making the product safer than powders or sprays.

Chemical Contamination is a substance that has come in contact with food and can cause foodborne illness. There are many potential sources, such as cleaners, sanitizers, pesticides, and even food ingredients (e.g., food preservatives) if not used currently.

Chemical Sanitizing is a method of disinfecting surfaces to prevent pathogenic cross-contamination. Microorganisms must contact the chemical agent for a minimum time to be neutralized. Surfaces cleaned with chemicals must be adequately rinsed and wiped to avoid the chemical becoming a food contaminant. Typical options used are chlorine, quaternary ammonia, and iodine.

Chlorine is a widely used chemical in foodservice to sanitize surfaces and equipment by killing bacteria. A sanitizer solution with a concentration of 50—99 ppm must contact a surface for at least 7 seconds to kill pathogens effectively.

Ciguatera Fish Poisoning is an illness caused by eating fish that contain toxins produced by a marine microalgae called Gambierdiscus toxicus. People with ciguatera may experience nausea, vomiting, and neurologic symptoms such as tingling fingers or toes.

Clean describes an object or surface with no signs of dirt or stains. Clean does not mean sanitized, which has to do with reducing pathogens to safe levels. However, a surface must be cleaned before it may be adequately sanitized.

Cleaned in Place (CIP) involves a mechanical system used to clean the inner workings of food equipment without the need to disassemble it, such as a frozen dessert machine. In this example, the food product is emptied and replaced (by the CIP system) with a detergent solution, a water rinse, and then a sanitizing solution. CIP does not include the cleaning of equipment such as band saws, slicers, or mixers that are subjected to in-place manual cleaning without the use of a CIP system.

Cleaning Agent describes a chemical compound used to remove food, dirt, and stains from surfaces.

Clostridium Botulinum (C. botulinum) is a spore-forming bacterium that produces a deadly neurotoxin in food when time-temperature abused. Notably, growth can occur without oxygen but is limited in highly acidic food or refrigeration. Botulism is a severe form of foodborne illness with a high mortality rate.

Clostridium Perfringens (C. perfringens) is a spore-forming bacteria commonly found in meats, poultry, and raw vegetables. Spores produced by C. perfringens are resistant to high temperatures often resulting in the presence of this bacteria even after cooking. Time-temperature abuse of these cooked foods promotes bateria growth, leading to foodborne illness.

Cold-holding Equipment is designed to keep foods for service out of the temperature danger zone, maintaining 41°F (5°C) or colder.

Commercial refers to food-related businesses or establishments that transport, sell, or provide food meant for consumers – not food prepared at home for personal consumption. It can also mean professional quality NSF-approved foodservice equipment rather than residential-grade.

Commingle means the act of combining different lots of shellfish.

Comminuted means reduced in size by methods including chopping, flaking, grinding, or mincing. It also describes fish or meat products that are reduced in size and restructured or reformulated such as gefilte fish, gyros, ground beef, and sausage; and a mixture of two or more types of meat that have been reduced in size and combined, such as sausages.

Conditional Employee is a potential food employee to whom a job offer is made, conditional on responses to subsequent medical questions or examinations designed to identify potential food employees who may be suffering from a disease that can be transmitted through food and done in compliance with Title 1 of the Americans with Disabilities Act of 1990.

Confirmed Disease Outbreak is a foodborne disease outbreak in which laboratory analysis of appropriate specimens identifies a causative agent and epidemiological analysis implicates the food as the source of the illness.

Consumer is a person who is a member of the public, takes possession of food, is not functioning in the capacity of an operator of a food establishment or food processing plant, and does not offer the food for resale.

Contact Spray are chemicals (power or liquid) used to control insects by killing them, preventing them from contaminating food, or engaging in undesirable or destructive behaviors.

Contamination introduces physical, chemical, or biological substances in food or a beverage. These substances are often harmful and can lead to foodborne illness if consumed. The cause of the contamination can be intentional (intent to cause harm), unintentional (accidental cross-contamination), or naturally occurring (a chemical reaction between food and metal pan/container).

Control Measures describe actions taken by a pest control operator (PCO) to remove or destroy harmful infestations, such as insects or rodents, within a foodservice establishment to help prevent foodborne illnesses from contaminated food.

Cooling Coils are tubes that contain refrigerant used to create cold air within freezers, refrigerators, and HVAC equipment. These coils should be kept clean for optimal performance (for both energy and temperature). To maintain a healthy environment (free of mold and mildew) and to protect food (stored or prepared) any condensation created from this process should be properly captured and drained.

Core Item refers to a provision in the FDA Food Code that is not designated as a "priority item" or a "priority foundation item". A "core item" includes an item that usually relates to general sanitation, operational controls, sanitation standard operating procedures (SSOPs), facilities or structures, equipment design, or general maintenance.

Corrective Action is an immediate intervention based on the food establishment's hazard analysis critical control point (HACCP) plan. Examples are disposing of contaminated food, reheating food within its critical control point (CCP,) or retraining a food employee on correct handwashing procedures.

Corrosion-resistant Material is a material that maintains acceptable surface cleanability characteristics under the prolonged influence of the food to be contacted, the normal use of cleaning compounds and sanitizing solutions, and other conditions of the use environment.

Counter-mounted Equipment is equipment that is not portable and is designed to be mounted off the floor on a table, counter, or shelf.

Coving describes the curved edge created between the floor and wall, usually by the floor material (resilient or tile) continuing up the wall. The curved, or coved, edge is easier to clean than a 90-degree corner.

Critical Control Point (CCP) is a point or procedure in a specific food system where the loss of control may result in an unacceptable health risk to the consumer. Identifying when hazards may occur is an essential part of an HACCP plan.

Critical Limit is the maximum or minimum value to which a physical, biological, or chemical parameter must be controlled at a <u>critical control point</u> to minimize the <u>risk</u> that the identified food safety <u>hazard</u> may occur.

Cross Connection describes a physical connection between drinkable water and a liquid or gas that could make the water unsafe to drink. Wherever there is a cross-connection, there is a potential threat to public health from the liquid or gas contaminants. This prohibited condition applies to permanent (e.g. an installed pipe) and temporary (a hose running from a faucet to a mop bucket containing dirty water) connections.

Cross-Contact occurs when allergens are transferred to a food which does not contain the allergen by the actions of a food employee.

Cross-Contamination occurs when a pathogen, chemical, or physical substance has been transferred to a food or beverage. The result can be potentially harmful, causing foodborne illness if consumed.

Crustacea are aquatic arthropods (with four or more pairs of limbs), including lobster, shrimp, and crab.

Cut leafy greens describe fresh leafy greens whose leaves have been cut, shredded, sliced, chopped, or torn. The term "leafy greens" includes iceberg lettuce, romaine lettuce, leaf lettuce, butter lettuce, baby leaf lettuce (i.e., immature lettuce or leafy greens), escarole, endive, spring mix, spinach, cabbage, kale, arugula, and chard. The term "leafy greens" does not include herbs such as cilantro or parsley.

Danger zone is the food-holding temperature range between 41°F and 135°F (5°C and 57°C) which supports the growth of pathogenic microorganisms.

Dealer means a <u>person</u> who is authorized by a <u>shellfish control authority</u> for the activities of <u>shellstock</u> shipper, shucker-packer, repacker, reshipper, or depuration processor of <u>molluscan shellfish</u> according to the provisions of the National Shellfish Sanitation Program.

Detergent is a cleaning agent used to loosen and remove dirt and impurities from a surface.

Disclosure means a written statement that clearly identifies the animal-derived foods which are, or can be ordered, raw, undercooked, or without otherwise being processed to eliminate pathogens, or items that contain an ingredient that is raw, undercooked, or without otherwise being processed to eliminate pathogens.

Drinking Water means water that meets criteria as specified in 40 CFR 141 National Primary Drinking Water Regulations. Drinking water is traditionally known as potable water. Drinking water includes the term "water" except where the term used connotes that the water is not potable, such as "boiler water," "mop water," "rainwater," "wastewater," and "nondrinking" water.

Dry storage area means a room or area designated for the storage of packaged or containerized bulk food that is not <u>time/temperature control for safety food</u> and dry goods such as <u>single-service</u> items.

Easily Cleanable means a characteristic of a surface that: (a) Allows effective removal of soil by normal cleaning methods; (b) Is dependent on the material, design, construction, and installation of the surface; and (c) Varies with the likelihood of the surface's role in introducing pathogenic or toxigenic agents or other contaminants into food based on the surface's <u>approved</u> placement, purpose, and use.

Easily movable means: (1) Portable; mounted on casters, gliders, or rollers; or provided with a mechanical means to safely tilt a unit of <u>equipment</u> for cleaning; and (2) Having no utility connection, a utility connection that disconnects quickly, or a flexible utility connection line of sufficient length to allow the <u>equipment</u> to be moved for cleaning of the <u>equipment</u> and adjacent area.

Egg means the shell egg of avian species such as chicken, duck, goose, guinea, quail, <u>ratites</u> or turkey. Not included in the definition of egg: (a) A <u>balut</u>; (b) The egg of reptile species such as alligator; or (c) An <u>egg product</u>.

Egg Product describes all, or a portion of, the contents found inside <u>eggs</u> separated from the shell and pasteurized in a <u>food processing plant</u>, with or without added ingredients, intended for human consumption, such as dried, frozen, or liquid eggs. Egg Product does not include food that only contains a relatively small proportion of eggs, such as cake mixes.

Employee means the <u>permit holder</u>, <u>person in charge</u>, <u>food employee</u>, a <u>person</u> having supervisory or management duties, a <u>person</u> on the payroll, family member, volunteer, a <u>person</u> performing work under contractual agreement, or other <u>person</u> working in a <u>food establishment</u>.

EPA means the U.S. Environmental Protection Agency.

Equipment means an article that is used in the operation of a <u>food establishment</u> such as a freezer, grinder, hood, ice maker, <u>meat</u> block, mixer, oven, reach-in refrigerator, scale, sink, slicer, stove, table, <u>temperature measuring device</u> for ambient air, <u>vending machine</u>, or <u>warewashing</u> machine. The term equipment does not include apparatuses used for handling or storing large quantities of <u>packaged foods</u> that are received from a supplier in a cased or overwrapped lot, such as hand trucks, forklifts, dollies, pallets, racks, and skids.

Exclude means to prevent a <u>person</u> from working as an <u>employee</u> in a <u>food establishment</u> or entering a <u>food establishment</u> as an <u>employee</u>. An excluded person cannot be prevented from entering areas open to the public within a food establishment.

Expiration Date is the date after which a food product is not at its optimal quality according to the manufacturer.

FAT TOM is a mnemonic device that describes the favorable intrinsic and extrinsic conditions of food that foodborne bacteria need to grow: food, acidity, temperature, time, oxygen, and moisture.

FDA Food Code is a best practice safety regulation for food operations and employees developed by the U.S. government. The Food Code is not mandated but is recommended for adoption by state, county, local, and tribal municipalities to promote safety for employees and consumers.

Fecal-oral route is a means of spreading pathogenic microorganisms from feces produced by an infected host to another host, usually via the mouth; e.g., contact between contaminated hands or objects and the mouth.

Feces is the waste that's passed out of the body after food has gone through the bowel.

First-in, First-out (FIFO) storage method describes a storage rotation method that ensures the oldest products are used or consumed first, based on the expiration date. This helps prevent stored products from expiring or spoiling due to always being on the back of the shelf.

Fish means fresh or saltwater finfish, crustaceans, and other forms of aquatic life (including alligator, frog, aquatic turtle, jellyfish, sea cucumber, and sea urchin and the roe of such animals) other than birds or mammals, and all mollusks, if such animal life is intended for human consumption. The term fish also includes an edible human food product derived in whole or in part from fish, including fish that have been processed in any manner.

Food means a raw, cooked, or processed edible substance, ice, <u>beverage</u>, or ingredient used or intended for use or for sale in whole or in part for human consumption, or chewing gum.

Foodborne Illness is an illness caused by a harmful contaminant in consumed food.

Food and Drug Administration (FDA) is a U.S. government agency responsible for protecting public health by ensuring the safety of the nation's food supply. The FDA created and continues to maintain the <u>FDA Food Code</u>.

Foodborne disease outbreak or foodborne illness outbreak means the occurrence of two or more cases of a similar illness resulting from the ingestion of a common food.

Food-contact Surface describes a surface of <u>equipment</u> or a <u>utensil</u> with which food normally comes into contact; or a surface of <u>equipment</u> or a <u>utensil</u> from which food may drain, drip, or splash into a food, or onto a surface normally in contact with food.

Food Defense Program describes an establishment's internal program to protect food products from intentional contamination by an employee, consumer, or public, where there is an intent to cause public health harm.

Food Safety Management System is a foundational system developed and implemented by <u>food establishment</u> operators to ensure food handling practices reduce the risk of foodborne illness and ensure the safest products possible.

Food employee means an individual working with unpackaged food, food equipment or utensils, or food-contact surfaces.

Food Establishment means an operation that: (a) stores, prepares, packages, serves, vends food directly to the consumer, or otherwise provides food for human consumption such as a restaurant; satellite or catered feeding location; catering operation if the operation provides food directly to a consumer or to a conveyance used to transport people; market; vending location; conveyance used to transport people; institution; or food bank; and (b) relinquishes possession of food to a consumer directly, or indirectly through a delivery service such as home delivery of grocery orders or restaurant takeout orders, or delivery service that is provided by common carriers. This includes: (a) An element of the operation such as a transportation vehicle or a central preparation facility that supplies a vending location or satellite feeding location unless the vending or feeding location is permitted by the regulatory authority; and (b) An operation that is conducted in a mobile, stationary, temporary, or permanent facility or location; where consumption is on or off the premises; and regardless of whether there is a charge for the food.

Food preparation process means a process using raw animal or plant food, ready-to-eat foods, and other ingredients that produce a ready-to-eat food, safe for consumption.

Food Processing Plant means a commercial operation that manufactures, packages, labels, or stores food for human consumption, and provides food for sale or distribution to other business entities such as food processing plants or food establishments. It does not include a food establishment.

Freshwater means inland water, such as lakes, rivers, streams, and ponds. Some parasites (see definition) that live in freshwater can cause illness in humans if the water is used for drinking or for watering or rinsing fruits and vegetables, for example.

Fungi means eukaryotic, diverse, widespread unicellular and multicellular organisms that lack chlorophyll, usually bear spores, and may be filamentous. Examples of fungi include yeasts, molds, and mushrooms.

Game Animal means an animal, the products of which are food, that is not classified as livestock, sheep, swine, goat, horse, mule, or other equine, or as poultry, or fish. Also included are mammals such as reindeer, elk, deer, antelope, water buffalo, bison, rabbit, squirrel, opossum, raccoon, nutria, or muskrat, and nonaquatic reptiles such as land snakes. Game animal does not include ratites.

General use pesticide means a pesticide that is not classified by EPA for restricted use as specified in 40 CFR 152.175 Pesticides classified for restricted use.

Grade A standards means the requirements of the United States Public Health Service/FDA Grade A Pasteurized Milk Ordinance with which certain fluid and dry milk and milk products comply.

HACCP plan means a written document that delineates the formal procedures for following the hazard analysis and critical control point principles developed by The National Advisory Committee on Microbiological Criteria for Foods.

Hair restraint means a device used to prevent a food employee's head, facial, or body hair from contaminating food.

Handwashing Sink means a lavatory, a basin or vessel for washing, a wash basin, or a plumbing fixture especially placed for use in personal hygiene and designed for the washing of the hands. It also includes an automatic handwashing facility.

Hand antiseptic consists of sprays, gels, or wipes that can kill many harmful bacterial cells (but not spores — see definition). The alcohol in hand sanitizers doesn't destroy norovirus, the leading cause of foodborne illness in the U.S. Handwashing is the best prevention.

Hazard means a biological, chemical, or physical property that may cause an unacceptable consumer health risk.

Health practitioner means a physician licensed to practice medicine, or if allowed by law, a nurse practitioner, physician assistant, or similar medical professional.

Hazard analysis and critical control point (HACCP) means a prevention-based food safety system that identifies and monitors specific food safety hazards that can adversely affect the safety of food products.

Health inspector means a person representing the authority having jurisdiction (AHJ), such as state, county, city, and tribal employees, who perform surprise inspections of food establishments to ensure food is safe for consumption.

Hermetically sealed container means a container that is designed and intended to be secure against the entry of microorganisms and, in the case of low acid canned foods, to maintain the commercial sterility of its contents after processing.

Highly susceptible population (HSP) or high risk population means persons who are more likely than other people in the general population to experience foodborne disease because they are: (1) Immunocompromised; preschool age children, or older adults; and (2) Obtaining food at a facility that provides services such as custodial care, health care, or assisted living, such as a child or adult day care center, kidney dialysis center, hospital or nursing home, or nutritional or socialization services such as a senior center.

Hygiene means behaviors that prevent disease and help people stay healthy. Examples of hygienic behaviors include handwashing, using clean cooking equipment, and keeping kitchen counters clean.

Ice-point method Thermometer calibration method based on the freezing point of water, which is 32 F (0 C).

Imminent health hazard means a significant threat or danger to health that is considered to exist when there is evidence sufficient to show that a product, practice, circumstance, or event creates a situation that requires immediate correction or cessation of operation to prevent injury based on: (1) The number of potential injuries, and (2) The nature, severity, and duration of the anticipated injury.

Immune System The human body's ability to defend against illness. Individuals with a weak immune system are more prone to contracting a foodborne illness.

Infection means a bacterium, virus, or other pathogen enters the body and multiplies. The symptoms caused by the infection often are the result of the immune system's response to the pathogen, such as inflammation. Infections may spread out of the site in which they first entered and grow in the body; for example, foodborne pathogens occasionally spread from the bowel into the bloodstream and into other organs.

Injected means injecting a solution into meat by processes that are referred to as "injecting," "pump marinating," or "stitch pumping".

In-Shell Product means non-living, processed shellfish with one or both shells present.

Intact Meat means a cut of whole muscle(s) meat that has not undergone comminution, mechanical tenderization, vacuum tumbling with solutions, reconstruction, cubing, or pounding. The 2022 Food Code calls these modifications "nonIntact Meat" in 3-401.11(A)(2).

Integrated Pest Management is a science-based decision-making process that combines tools and strategies to identify and manage pests.

Internal temperature means the temperature of the thickest part of the food internally.

Jaundice is a medical condition, possibly a symptom of foodborne illness, resulting in the yellowing of the skin and the whites of the eyes.

Juice means the aqueous liquid expressed or extracted from one or more fruits or vegetables, purées of the edible portions of one or more fruits or vegetables, or any concentrates of such liquid or purée. It does not include, for purposes of HACCP, liquids, purées, or concentrates that are not used as beverages or ingredients of beverages.

Kitchenware means food preparation and storage utensils.

Law means applicable local, state, tribal, and federal statutes, regulations, and ordinances.

Linens means fabric items such as cloth hampers, cloth napkins, table cloths, wiping cloths, and work garments including cloth gloves.

Log-phase is an exponential increase by a factor of 10 in bacterial growth.

Major Food Allergen means: (a) milk, egg, fish (such as bass, flounder, cod), crustacean shellfish (such as crab, lobster, or shrimp), tree nuts (such as almonds, pecans, or walnuts), wheat, peanuts, soybeans, and sesame; or (b) a food ingredient that contains protein derived from the nine items just listed.

Meat means the flesh of animals used as food including the dressed flesh of cattle, swine, sheep, or goats and other edible animals, except fish, poultry, and wild game animals.

Mechanically Tenderized means manipulating meat by piercing with a set of needles, pins, blades or any mechanical device, which breaks up muscle fiber and tough connective tissue, to increase tenderness. This includes injection, scoring, and processes which may be referred to as "blade tenderizing," "jaccarding," "pinning," or "needling".

mg/L means milligrams per liter, which is the metric equivalent of parts per million (ppm).

Microorganism means a form of life that can be seen only with a microscope. These microorganisms can cause foodborne illness: bacteria, viruses, parasites, and fungi.

Minimum internal temperature means the temperature, for a certain amount of time, required to kill anticipated microbial load in a specific food product.

Mold means a type of fungus that contaminates food and causes spoilage or toxins leading to foodborne illness.

Molluscan shellfish means any edible species of fresh or frozen oysters, clams, mussels, and scallops or edible portions thereof, except when the scallop product consists only of the shucked adductor muscle. This includes shellstock, shucked shellfish and inshell products.

Monitoring results in the observation and taking of measurements to ascertain if critical limits are being maintained or met.

Mucus means the bowel is lined with mucus, a slippery substance that helps food pass through the bowel. In some foodborne illnesses that cause diarrhea, this mucus is passed with the feces.

Non-Continuous Cooking means the cooking of food in a food establishment using a process in which the initial heating of the food is intentionally halted so that it may be cooled and held for complete cooking at a later time prior to sale or service. It does not include cooking procedures that only involve temporarily interrupting or slowing an otherwise continuous cooking process.

Non-food contact surface is a surface food is not allowed to contact or be prepared on, for example, the top of a microwave, a single-service utensil storage shelf, or a floor.

NSF International is a non-profit organization with a mission to improve global health through the development of standards and certifications that protect food, water, products, and the environment.

Off-site service means catering and vending activities located away from where the food was originally prepared and cooked.

Outbreak happens when two or more people become sick from the same bacterium, virus, or other pathogen. When outbreaks of illness from foods regulated by the Food and Drug Administration (FDA) occur, the FDA, the Centers for Disease Control and Prevention, and state health authorities investigate together, to find the source of the contaminated food that caused the illness, so that the outbreak can be stopped.

Operational step means a step or procedure within the flow of food such as receiving, storage, preparation, serving, or warewashing.

Packaged means bottled, canned, cartoned, bagged, or wrapped, whether packaged in a food establishment or a food processing plant. It does not include wrapped or placed in a carry-out container to protect the food during service or delivery to the consumer, by a food employee, upon consumer request.

Parasite means certain amoebas and worms that can be passed to humans (and to other animals, in most cases) in contaminated food or water; once inside humans, they use the human's resources to sustain them, without helping the human in any way. Some make the human sick. Some parasites die naturally in a short time and are passed out of the body. Others, such as tapeworms, can live in the human bowel for years. Most parasites that affect humans are too small to be seen with the naked eye. Worms that affect humans are too small to be seen with the naked eye at the life stage when they can cause an infection, but grow larger inside humans. Water, soil, and hands that are contaminated with feces from an infected person – even particles too small to see – are common ways that parasites are passed into the mouths of humans.

Pasteurization is a process used on some foods and drinks, by food manufacturers, to kill the kinds and amounts of bacteria that can cause illness. Pasteurization applies a certain amount of heat for a certain amount of time, depending on the type of food or drink and the bacteria that are able to live and grow in it. Pasteurization isn't appropriate for some foods. And even though a food may be pasteurized, it still has to be stored properly afterwards; otherwise, harmful bacteria could grow in it.

Milk is one example of how pasteurization helps keep foods safe. *Un*pasteurized ("raw") milk and certain cheeses made from raw milk can contain harmful amounts of bacteria, such as the types of *E. coli*, *Listeria*, and *Brucella* that cause illness. Even though *un*pasteurized milk has caused many illnesses and even has resulted in deaths, some people claim that it's healthier than pasteurized milk. There's no scientific evidence to support this.

Pathogen means a life form, such as a bacterium or protozoan, that can cause disease. Viruses are not life forms, but some cause disease and are among the pathogens.

Permit means the document issued by the regulatory authority that authorizes a person to operate a food establishment.

Permit holder means the entity that (1) Is legally responsible for the operation of the food establishment such as the owner, the owner's agent, or other person; and (2) Possesses a valid permit to operate a food establishment.

Person means an association, a corporation, individual, partnership, other legal entity, government, or governmental subdivision or agency.

Person in charge means the individual present at a food establishment who is responsible for the operation at the time of inspection.

Personal Care Items means items or substances that may be poisonous, toxic, or a source of contamination and are used to maintain or enhance a person's health, hygiene, or appearance. This includes items such as medicines; first aid supplies; and other items such as cosmetics, and toiletries such as toothpaste and mouthwash.

Pest Control Operator means a licensed professional with special training and products for use within a food service establishment.

Pesticides means a substance, that is harmful to plants and animals, used to destroy insects and other organisms.

pH means the symbol for the negative logarithm of the hydrogen ion concentration, which is a measure of the degree of acidity or alkalinity of a solution. Values between 0 and 7 indicate acidity and values between 7 and 14 indicate alkalinity. The value for pure distilled water is 7, which is considered neutral.

Physical facilities means the structure and interior surfaces of a food establishment including accessories such as soap and towel dispensers and attachments such as light fixtures and heating or air conditioning system vents.

Plumbing fixture means a receptacle or device that: (1) Is permanently or temporarily connected to the water distribution system of the premises and demands a supply of water from the system; or (2) Discharges used water, waste materials, or sewage directly or indirectly to the drainage system of the premises.

Plumbing system means the water supply and distribution pipes; plumbing fixtures and traps; soil, waste, and vent pipes; sanitary and storm sewers and building drains, including their respective connections, devices, and appurtenances within the premises; and water-treating equipment.

Poisonous or toxic materials means substances that are not intended for ingestion and are included in 4 categories: (1) Cleaners and sanitizers, which include cleaning and sanitizing agents and agents such as caustics, acids, drying agents, polishes, and other chemicals; (2) Pesticides, except sanitizers, which include substances such as insecticides and rodenticides; (3) Substances necessary for the operation and maintenance of the establishment such as nonfood grade lubricants and personal care items that may be deleterious to health; and (4) Substances that are not necessary for the operation and maintenance of the establishment and are on the premises for retail sale, such as petroleum products and paints. (5) Restricted use pesticide means a pesticide product that contains the active ingredients specified in 40 CFR 152.175 Pesticides classified for restricted use, and that is limited to use by or under the direct supervision of a certified applicator

Potable means water that is safe to drink. Water from the tap is almost always potable in the U.S.

Poultry means: (1) Any domesticated bird (chickens, turkeys, ducks, geese, guineas, ratites, or squabs), whether live or dead, and (2) Any migratory waterfowl or game bird, pheasant, partridge, quail, grouse, or pigeon, whether live or dead.

Premises means: (1) The physical facility, its contents, and the contiguous land or property under the control of the permit holder; or (2) The physical facility, its contents, and the land or property not described in Subparagraph (1) of this definition if its facilities and contents are under the control of the permit holder and may impact food establishment personnel, facilities, or operations, and a food establishment is only one component of a larger operation such as a health care facility, hotel, motel, school, recreational camp, or prison.

Primal cut means a basic major cut into which carcasses and sides of meat are separated, such as a beef round, pork loin, lamb flank, or veal breast.

Priority Item means a provision in the FDA Food Code whose application contributes directly to the elimination, prevention, or reduction to an acceptable level, hazards associated with foodborne illness or injury and there is no other provision that more directly controls the hazard. This includes items with a quantifiable measure to show control of hazards such as cooking, reheating, cooling, handwashing; and A Priority Item is an item that is denoted in the Food Code with a superscript P.

Priority Foundation Item means a provision in the FDA Food Code whose application supports, facilitates, or enables one or more priority items. This includes an item that requires the purposeful incorporation of specific actions, equipment, or procedures by industry management to attain control of risk factors that contribute to foodborne illness or injury such as personnel training, infrastructure or necessary equipment, HACCP plans, documentation, or record keeping, and labeling; and is an item that is denoted in the Food Code with a superscript Pf.

Public water system means a municipal entity provides potable water as a public service. This service is typically delivered through public and private pressurized pipe networks.

Ratite means a flightless bird such as an emu, ostrich, or rhea.

Ready-to-Eat Food (RTE) means food that: (a) Is in a form that is edible without additional preparation to achieve food safety; or (b) Is a raw or partially cooked animal food and the consumer is advised; or (c) Is prepared in accordance with a variance that is granted; and (d) May receive additional preparation for palatability or aesthetic, epicurean, gastronomic, or culinary purposes.

Ready-to-eat food <u>includes</u> (a) Raw animal food that is cooked, or frozen; (b) Raw fruits and vegetables that are washed; (c) Plant foods that are cooked for hot holding; (d) All time/temperature control for safety (TCS) food that is cooked to the temperature and time required for the specific food; (e) Plant food for which further washing, cooking, or other processing is not required for food safety, and from which rinds, peels, husks, or shells, if naturally present are removed; (f) Substances derived from plants such as spices, seasonings, and sugar; (g) A bakery item such as bread, cakes, pies, fillings, or icing for which further cooking is not required for food safety; (h) The following products that are produced in accordance with USDA guidelines and that have received a lethality treatment for pathogens: dry, fermented sausages, such as dry salami or pepperoni; salt-cured meat and poultry products, such as prosciutto ham, country cured ham, and Parma ham; and dried meat and poultry products, such as jerky or beef sticks;

and (i) foods manufactured, Thermally Processed Low-Acid Foods Packaged in Hermetically Sealed Containers.

Ready-to-eat food <u>does not include</u> (a) commercially packaged food that bears a manufacturer's cooking instructions, and (b) food for which the manufacturer has provided information that it has not been processed to control pathogens.

Reduced Oxygen Packaging means: (1)(a) The reduction of the amount of oxygen in a package by removing oxygen; displacing oxygen and replacing it with another gas or combination of gases; or otherwise controlling the oxygen content to a level below that normally found in the atmosphere (approximately 21% at sea level); and (b) A process that involves a food for which the hazards Clostridium botulinum or Listeria monocytogenes require control in the final packaged form. (2) This includes: (a) Vacuum packaging, in which air is removed from a package of food and the package is hermetically sealed so that a vacuum remains inside the package; (b) Modified atmosphere packaging, in which the atmosphere of a package of food is modified so that its composition is different from air but the atmosphere may change over time due to the permeability of the packaging material or the respiration of the food. Modified atmosphere packaging includes reduction in the proportion of oxygen, total replacement of oxygen, or an increase in the proportion of other gases such as carbon dioxide or nitrogen; (c) Controlled atmosphere packaging, in which the atmosphere of a package of food is modified so that until the package is opened, its composition is different from air, and continuous control of that atmosphere is maintained, such as by using oxygen scavengers or a combination of total replacement of oxygen, nonrespiring food, and impermeable packaging material; (d) Cook chill packaging, in which cooked food is hot filled into impermeable bags that are then sealed or crimped closed. The bagged food is rapidly chilled and refrigerated at temperatures that inhibit the growth of psychrotrophic pathogens; or (e) Sous vide packaging, in which raw or partially cooked food is vacuum packaged in an impermeable bag, cooked in the bag, rapidly chilled, and refrigerated at temperatures that inhibit the growth of psychrotrophic pathogens.

Refuse means solid waste not carried by water through the sewage system.

Regulatory Authority means the tribal, local, state, or federal enforcement body or authorized representative having jurisdiction over the food establishment.

Reminder or **Consumer Advisory** means a written statement concerning the health risk of consuming animal foods raw, undercooked, or without otherwise being processed to eliminate pathogens.

Re-service means the transfer of food that is unused and returned by a consumer after being served or sold and in the possession of the consumer, to another person.

Restrict means to limit the activities of a food employee so that there is no risk of transmitting a disease that is transmissible through food and the food employee does not work with exposed food, clean equipment, UTENSILS, LINENS, or unwrapped single-service or single-use articles.

Restricted Egg means any check, dirty egg, incubator reject, inedible, leaker, or loss.

Restricted use pesticide means a pesticide product that contains the active ingredients specified in 40 CFR 152.175 Pesticides classified for restricted use, and that is limited to use by or under the direct supervision of a certified applicator.

Risk means the likelihood that an adverse health effect will occur within a population as a result of a hazard in a food.

Safe Material means an article manufactured from or composed of materials that may not reasonably be expected to result, directly or indirectly, in their becoming a component or otherwise affecting the characteristics of any food; (2) An additive that is used; or (3) Other materials that are not additives and that are used in conformity with applicable regulations of the Food and Drug Administration.

Sanitization is not the same as cleaning and involves the application of cumulative heat or chemicals on cleaned food-contact surfaces that, when evaluated for efficacy, is sufficient to yield a reduction of 5 logs, which is equal to a 99.999% reduction, of representative disease microorganisms of public health importance.

Scombroid poisoning, also known as histamine fish poisoning, is an allergic-type reaction that occurs within a few hours of eating fish contaminated with high levels of histamine.

Sealed means free of cracks or other openings that allow the entry or passage of moisture.

Service Animal means an animal such as a guide dog, signal dog, or other animals individually trained to provide assistance to an individual with a disability.

Servicing Area means an operating base location to which a mobile food establishment or transportation vehicle that returns regularly for such things as vehicle and equipment cleaning, discharging liquid or solid wastes, refilling water tanks and ice bins, and boarding food.

Sewage means liquid waste containing animal or vegetable matter in suspension or solution and may include liquids containing chemicals in solution.

Shellfish Control Authority means a state, federal, foreign, tribal, or other government entity legally responsible for administering a program that includes certification of molluscan shellfish harvesters and dealers for interstate commerce.

Shellstock means live molluscan shellfish in the shell.

Shell stock identification tag identifies the dealer and where the shellfish were purchased and is required.

Shiga Toxin-producing Escherichia coli (STEC) means any *E.coli* capable of producing *Shiga* toxins (also called verocytotoxins). STEC infections can be asymptomatic or may result in a spectrum of illnesses ranging from mild non-bloody diarrhea, to hemorrhagic colitis (i.e., bloody diarrhea), to hemolytic uremic syndrome (HUS - a type of kidney failure). Examples of serotypes of STEC include: E. coli O157:H7; E. coli O157:NM; E. coli O26:H11; E. coli O145:NM; E. coli O103:H2; and E. coli O111:NM. STEC are sometimes referred to as VTEC (verocytotoxigenic E. coli) or as EHEC (Enterohemorrhagic E. coli). EHEC are a subset of STEC which can cause hemorrhagic colitis or HUS.

Shucked shellfish means molluscan shellfish that have <u>both</u> shells removed.

Single-service articles mean tableware, carry-out utensils, and other items such as bags, containers, placemats, stirrers, straws, toothpicks, and wrappers that are designed and constructed for one time, one person use after which they are intended for discard.

Single-Use Articles means utensils and bulk food containers designed and constructed to be used once and discarded. This includes items such as wax paper, butcher paper, plastic wrap, formed aluminum food containers, jars, plastic tubs or buckets, bread wrappers, pickle barrels, ketchup bottles, and number 10 cans.

Single-Use Gloves are latex or latex alternative gloves designed for single use and intended to protect food from cross-contamination caused by bare hand contact.

Slacking is the process of moderating the temperature of a food such as allowing a food to gradually increase from a temperature of -10° F (-23° C) to 25°F (-4°C) in preparation for deep-fat frying or to facilitate even heat penetration during the cooking of previously block-frozen food such as shrimp.

Spore (endospore) means a few bacteria, including some that can cause foodborne illness, can produce inactive forms called endospores. The bacteria do this when their survival is threatened; for example, when there is very little or no nutrition available to them. Endospores can exist for many years and in very tough conditions. They don't need nutrition and can withstand heat, freezing, and disinfectants. When conditions improve, the spores become active bacteria again. Like bacteria, endospores can contaminate food and water.

Tableware any eating, drinking, or serving utensils for table use such as flatware including forks, knives, and spoons; hollowware including bowls, cups, serving dishes, and tumblers; and plates.

Temperature Measuring Device is a thermometer, thermocouple, thermistor, or other device that indicates the temperature of food, air, or water.

Temperature danger zone means a temperature range in which foodborne microorganisms grow rapidly; 41° F to 135° F (5° C to 57° C).

Temporary Food Establishment is a food establishment that operates for a period of no more than 14 consecutive days in conjunction with a single event or celebration.

Thermistors is an electrical resistor used to measure temperature.

Time/Temperature Abuse happens when food is not held at the correct temperature, for a certain amount of time, to limit the growth of pathogens.

Time/Temperature Control for Safety Food (TCS Food) (formerly "potentially hazardous food" or PHF)

(1) "Time/temperature control for safety food" means a food that requires time/temperature control for safety (TCS) to limit pathogenic microorganism growth or toxin formation.

(2) "Time/temperature control for safety food" includes: (a) An animal food that is raw or heat-treated; a plant FOOD that is heat treated or consists of raw seed sprouts, cut melons, cut leafy greens, cut tomatoes or mixtures of cut tomatoes that are not modified in a way so that they are unable to support pathogenic microorganism growth or toxin formation, or garlic-in-oil mixtures that are not modified in a way so that they are unable to support pathogenic microorganism growth or toxin formation; and (b) Except as specified in Subparagraph (3)(d) of this definition, a food that because of the interaction of its A.W. and P.H. values is designated as Product Assessment Required (P.A.)

(3) "Time/temperature control for safety food" does not include: (a) An air-cooled hard-boiled EGG with shell intact, or an egg with shell intact that is not hard-boiled, but has been pasteurized to destroy all viable salmonellae; (b) A food in an unopened hermetically sealed container that is commercially processed to achieve and maintain commercial sterility under conditions of non-refrigerated storage and distribution; (c) A food that because of its P.H. or A.W. value, or interaction of A.W. and P.H. values, is designated as a non-TCS food; (d) A food that is designated as Product Assessment Required (P.A.); or (e) A food that does not support the growth or toxin formation of pathogenic microorganisms.

Tobacco Product has the meaning stated in the Federal Food, Drug and Cosmetic Act §201(rr) (21 U.S.C. 321(rr)), which states: any product made or derived from tobacco, or containing nicotine from any source, that is intended for human consumption, including any component, part, or accessory of a tobacco product (except for raw materials other than tobacco used in manufacturing a component, part, or accessory of a tobacco product).

Toxins means a natural poison made by a living thing; for example, the toxins made by some bacteria. Venoms are toxins injected by animals.

U.S. Department of Agriculture (USDA) is an agency of the U.S. federal government responsible for inspecting meat, poultry, and eggs that cross state lines.

Utensil is a food-contact implement or container used in the storage, preparation, transportation, dispensing, sale, or service of food, such as kitchenware or tableware that is multiuse, single-service, or single-use; gloves used in contact with food; temperature sensing probes of food temperature measuring devices; and probe-type price or identification tags used in contact with food.

Validation means an implemented HACCP plan is working as designed by reviewing records and required steps in the plan to effectively control hazards to food.

Variance means a written document issued by the regulatory authority that authorizes a modification or waiver of one or more requirements of the Food Code if, in the opinion of the regulatory authority, a health hazard or nuisance will not result from the modification or waiver.

Vending Machine means a self-service device that, upon insertion of a coin, paper currency, token, card, or key, or by optional manual operation, dispenses unit servings of food in bulk or in packages without the necessity of replenishing the device between each vending operation.

Vending Machine Location means the room, enclosure, space, or area where one or more vending machines are installed and operated and includes the storage areas and areas on the premises that are used to service and maintain the vending machines.

Verification means ensuring the required steps of an implemented HACCP plan are executed at the critical control point.

Virus means a non-living entity that requires a host to survive and replicate. The virus offers no benefit to the host, can grow rapidly, cause sickness, and be potentially fatal in some cases.

Warewashing means the cleaning and sanitizing of utensils and food-contact surfaces of equipment.

Water Hardness is the amount of dissolved calcium and magnesium in the water which can affect the normal operation of equipment and the effectiveness of detergents.

Whole-muscle, Intact Beef means whole-muscle beef that is not injected, mechanically tenderized, reconstructed, or scored and marinated, from which beef steaks may be cut.

Yeast means a type of fungus capable of turning sugar into carbon dioxide and alcohol.

SDC PUBLICATIONS **What are the five handwashing steps?**	Lid
SDC PUBLICATIONS **When can a hand antiseptic be used?**	Immunocompromised Elderly Young children
SDC PUBLICATIONS **Which food may not be touched with bare hands?**	Restricted
SDC PUBLICATIONS **What is a ready-to-eat (RTE) food?**	Excluded
SDC PUBLICATIONS **Single-use gloves must be used when handling?**	An illness caused by a harmful substance in consumed food

SDC PUBLICATIONS **A food handler may have a beverage while working if it has a _____?**	1. Rinse 2. Soap 3. Rub 4. Rinse 5. Dry
SDC PUBLICATIONS **Highly susceptible populations (HPS) include?**	Only after washing hands
SDC PUBLICATIONS **A food handler who reports symptoms of an infected wound or cut must be _____ from work.**	Ready-to-eat (RTE) foods
SDC PUBLICATIONS **A food handler who reports symptoms of vomiting or diarrhea must be _____ from work.**	Any food that can be eaten as is – it does not need to be washed or cooked
SDC PUBLICATIONS **Define foodborne illness.**	Ready-to-eat (RTE) foods

SDC PUBLICATIONS List the "Big 6" bad bugs.	Time Temperature
SDC PUBLICATIONS What is a bad bug?	Temperature Danger Zone (TDZ)
SDC PUBLICATIONS Name the three living bad bugs covered in the coursebook.	False
SDC PUBLICATIONS Name the three non-living bad bugs covered in the coursebook.	Washing hands
SDC PUBLICATIONS Name each item associated with the mnemonic device FAT TOM.	True

SDC PUBLICATIONS **Name the two elements of FAT TOM that are always controllable.**	1. Hepatitis A 2. Norovirus 3. Salmonella spp. 4. Salmonella Typhi 5. E. coli 6. Shigella spp.
SDC PUBLICATIONS **Bacteria thrive in the** _____ _____ _____	A microorganism or naturally occurring contaminant that, at certain levels of concentration, causes foodborne illness in consumed food
SDC PUBLICATIONS **True or False,** **A toxin is a living substance.**	Bacteria Fungi Parasites
SDC PUBLICATIONS **A common preventative measure to bad bugs.**	Viruses Spores Toxins
SDC PUBLICATIONS **True or False,** **Some parasites can be seen with the naked eye.**	1. Food 2. Acidity 3. Temperature 4. Time 5. Oxygen 6. Moisture

List the types of contaminants.	Peanuts, Milk, Fish, Tree nuts, Eggs, Crustation Shellfish, Wheat, Soybeans, Sesame
What are the two primary sources of contaminants?	Occurs when allergens are transferred to a food that does not contain the allergen, by the actions of a food employee
What type of contaminant is wood, insulation, and dirt?	An allergic reaction to an allergen that can be severe or fatal to some
What is the danger of storing orange juice or lemonade in a pewter vessel/pitcher?	Produce
True or false, **Food allergens are naturally occurring chemicals.**	Follow Inspect Recognize Secure Tell

SDC PUBLICATIONS List the "Big 9" major food allergens.	1. Biological 2. Physical 3. Chemical 4. Naturally Occurring Chemical 5. Allergen
SDC PUBLICATIONS Define cross-contact.	People and food
SDC PUBLICATIONS Define Anaphylaxis.	Physical
SDC PUBLICATIONS What is a green cutting board used for cutting?	Chemical reaction/poisoning
SDC PUBLICATIONS Describe each aspect of the FIRST food defense program.	True

SDC PUBLICATIONS **What is the temperature range of the temperature danger zone?**	Bimetallic Stemmed Thermocouple and Thermistor Infrared Candy/Deep Fryer
SDC PUBLICATIONS **What does TCS stand for?**	Infrared
SDC PUBLICATIONS **Define TCS foods.**	Boiling water method Ice and water method
SDC PUBLICATIONS **What is the temperature range that supports rapid bacterial growth?**	Logs
SDC PUBLICATIONS **List some examples of TCS foods.**	Receiving Storage Cooking Reheating Hot holding Cold holding Cleaning

List the main types of thermometers.

41°F and 135°F (5°C–57°C)

Which thermometer measures the surface temperature?

Time/Temperature Control for Safety

What are the two methods of calibrating a bimetallic stemmed thermometer?

A food that requires time and/or temperature control for safety (TCS) to limit pathogenic growth or toxin formation

---

The only way to carefully monitor time is to track it in _____ .

70°F–125°F (21°C–52°C)

List some examples of when to measure food temperature.

An animal food that is raw or heat-treated, a plant food that is heat-treated, raw seed sprouts, cut melon, cut leafy greens, garlic in oil, cut tomatoes or mixtures of cut tomatoes

SDC PUBLICATIONS	
One of the world's most extensive laws of its kind?	90

SDC PUBLICATIONS	
_____ must be purchased from sources that comply with Grade A standards.	45°F (7°C) or below

SDC PUBLICATIONS	
_____ picked in the wild shall not be offered for sale or service by a food establishment.	135°F (57°C) or above

SDC PUBLICATIONS	
These two things are voluntary for a food manufacturer.	Frozen

SDC PUBLICATIONS	
Juice products that have not been pasteurized may not be served to _____ _____ _____.	Drinking or Potable

SDC PUBLICATIONS	
Tags for shellstock must be kept for _____ days.	Federal Food, Drug, and Cosmetic Act
SDC PUBLICATIONS	
Receiving temperature for milk and raw eggs?	Milk
SDC PUBLICATIONS	
Temperature for cooked TCS Foods received hot for service?	Mushrooms
SDC PUBLICATIONS	
Foods labeled and shipped frozen should be received _____.	Grading and Sell-by/Expiration Dates
SDC PUBLICATIONS	
Ice must be made from _____ water.	highly susceptible populations (HSP)

SDC PUBLICATIONS What does FIFO stand for?	False
SDC PUBLICATIONS Products must be stored _____ inches above the floor.	True
SDC PUBLICATIONS Refrigerated storage temperature must be?	Twenty-four
SDC PUBLICATIONS List some of the spaces food may not be stored in.	Seven
SDC PUBLICATIONS When storing food vertically, which food item must be on the bottom?	True

SDC PUBLICATIONS	
True or False, Pork should be stored above seafood.	First In First Out
True or False, The vertical storage order relates directly to the required internal cooking temperature.	Six
Date marking for TCS foods is required if held for more than _____ hours.	41°F (5°C) or below
Ready-to-eat TCS foods can be stored for a maximum of ___ days when properly refrigerated.	• Locker rooms • Toilet rooms • Dressing rooms • Garbage rooms • Mechanical rooms • Under sewer lines • Under leaking water lines
True or False, When combining foods, date-marking shall retain the date marking of the earliest food.	Poultry

SDC PUBLICATIONS True or False, The minimum internal temperature is more about taste than food safety.	145°F (63°C)
SDC PUBLICATIONS Frozen food must never be thawed at _____ _____.	155°F (68°C)
SDC PUBLICATIONS When thawing frozen food, it must never rise above what temperature?	165°F (73°C)
SDC PUBLICATIONS True or False, Do not wash precut or prewashed bagged produce.	Consumer Advisory
SDC PUBLICATIONS Minimum cooking temperature for plant-based food?	• From 135°F (57°C) to 70°F (21°C) within 2 hours, *and* • To 41°F (5°C) or below within 6 hours total

SDC PUBLICATIONS **Minimum cooking temperature for beef, pork, and shell eggs?**	False
SDC PUBLICATIONS **Minimum cooking temperature for ground meat and ratites?**	Room Temperature
SDC PUBLICATIONS **Minimum cooking temperature for poultry?**	41°F (5°C)
SDC PUBLICATIONS **Consumer notice that raw or undercooked state may be more likely to cause foodborne illness.**	True
SDC PUBLICATIONS **State the cooling temperature requirements for the first two hours, and then by six hours.**	135°F (57°C)

SDC PUBLICATIONS **Temperature requirement for hot holding for service?**	Eating, drinking, and serving utensils for the table
SDC PUBLICATIONS **Temperature requirement for cold holding for service?**	Food, Lips
SDC PUBLICATIONS **Maximum time allowed for hot holding without temperature control?**	Cleaned
SDC PUBLICATIONS **Requirements for cold holding without temperature control.**	Operates for a period of no more than 14 consecutive days in conjunction with a single event or celebration
SDC PUBLICATIONS **What is the temperature danger zone?**	True

SDC PUBLICATIONS	
Tableware means?	135°F (57°C) or above
SDC PUBLICATIONS	
Staff must not touch parts of tableware that come into contact with _____ or _____.	41°F (5°C) or below
SDC PUBLICATIONS	
In self-service areas, dispensers must be _____ prior to restocking.	Four hours
SDC PUBLICATIONS	
Define a temporary food establishment.	• Up to 4 hours (with no temperature monitoring) • Up to 6 hours if it never rises above 70°F (21°C).
SDC PUBLICATIONS	
True or False, Vending machines must have a self-closing door to prevent contamination in unattended areas.	41°F – 135°F (5°C – 57°C)

SDC PUBLICATIONS _____ is the process of removing visible organic matter and debris.	12.5 – 25 ppm
SDC PUBLICATIONS _____ is the process of destroying pathogenic microorganisms.	7 seconds
SDC PUBLICATIONS Define a food-contact surface.	Test kit, strips
SDC PUBLICATIONS True or False, Sanitization must happen before cleaning.	1. Wash 2. Rinse 3. Sanitize
SDC PUBLICATIONS What is the temperature and time required for hot water sanitization?	True

SDC PUBLICATIONS Iodine concentration requirement?	Cleaning
SDC PUBLICATIONS Minimum chlorine solution contact time?	Sanitizing
SDC PUBLICATIONS A sanitizing solution concentration should be verified using what?	A surface of equipment or a utensil that food normally comes into contact with or an adjacent surface where that food may drain, drip, or splash.
SDC PUBLICATIONS For a three-compartment sink, list the use of each sink, in order from left to right.	False
SDC PUBLICATIONS _____ towels may not be used to also clean up food spills.	171°F (77°C) for 30 seconds

SDC PUBLICATIONS **A business may not function as a food establishment until it has a** _____ ___ _____.	• Public water system • Private water system • Water transport vehicles • Water containers
SDC PUBLICATIONS **A** _____ _____ **must be in a separate enclosed space with a tight-sealing door.**	• Soap (one per two sinks minimum) • Hand drying provisions • Waste receptacle (if disposable towels are used) • Handwashing signage (one per sink)
SDC PUBLICATIONS _____ _____ **are required if staff routinely change clothes in the establishment.**	Air Gap
SDC PUBLICATIONS **Define "easily cleanable".**	1. 10 fc 2. 20 fc 3. 50 fc
SDC PUBLICATIONS **Name the areas carpet is not allowed.**	6 inches (15 cm) above a floor 4 inches (10 cm) above a countertop

SDC PUBLICATIONS **Approved sources for drinking water?**	Permit to Operate
SDC PUBLICATIONS **Handwashing sinks must have?**	Toilet Room
SDC PUBLICATIONS **What is the only fail-safe way to prevent backflow between the building's water supply and the sewage piping?**	Dressing Rooms
SDC PUBLICATIONS **List the footcandle requirements for storage, handwashing, and food preparation.**	• Allows effective removal of soil by normal cleaning methods • Is dependent on the material, design, construction, and installation of the surface
SDC PUBLICATIONS **What are the heights for equipment above a floor and a countertop?**	• Food preparation areas • Dishwashing areas • Toilet rooms • Garbage areas • Any area subject to moisture

SDC PUBLICATIONS **What is the distance rats travel from their nest?**	False
SDC PUBLICATIONS **What is the distance mice travel from their nest?**	Pest Control Operator (PCO)
SDC PUBLICATIONS **Flies are attracted to _____, predominantly _____ food.**	Integrated Pest Management (IPM)
SDC PUBLICATIONS **Animals are prohibited in food establishments, except for?**	Free of cracks or other openings that allow the entry or passage of moisture or pests
SDC PUBLICATIONS **Fish aquariums and display tanks are allowed in _____ areas.**	Feed Birds or Animals

SDC PUBLICATIONS True or False, Pest traps or bait stations may be placed above food if covered.	100 – 150 feet (30 – 46 m)
SDC PUBLICATIONS When dealing with pests, optimal results are obtained by working with a professional _____ _____ _____?	10 - 30 feet (3 – 9 m)
SDC PUBLICATIONS A science-based process that uses biological, environmental, and technological information to manage pest damage?	Food, Liquid
SDC PUBLICATIONS Define "sealed".	Service Animals
SDC PUBLICATIONS What should customers be reminded not to do in outdoor seating areas?	Customer

SDC PUBLICATIONS	
How many principles does an HACCP plan have?	• Demonstration of knowledge • Employee health controls • Controlling hands as a vehicle of contamination • Time and temperature parameters for controlling pathogens • Consumer advisory
SDC PUBLICATIONS	
The first principle of an HACCP plan?	Hazard Analysis Critical Control Point
SDC PUBLICATIONS	
What is the primary responsibility of the Person in Charge (PIC)?	Imminent health hazard
SDC PUBLICATIONS	
Written procedures are essential in controlling _____	A group of individuals who – collectively -- have complete knowledge of the operation should be identified to serve on a crisis management team in an emergency
SDC PUBLICATIONS	
Define "active managerial control".	Regulatory Authority

SDC PUBLICATIONS **Name the five FDA Public Health Interventions.**	Seven
SDC PUBLICATIONS **What does HACCP stand for?**	Hazard Analysis
SDC PUBLICATIONS **A food operation should be closed immediately if there is an _____ _____ _____?**	Compliance with the food code
SDC PUBLICATIONS **Define "crisis management team".**	Risk
SDC PUBLICATIONS **If operations are discontinued, permission shall be obtained from the _____ _____ before resuming operations.**	The PIC understands the law, knows staff have been properly trained, is aware of the various activities happening in the food establishment, and is always prepared for an inspection

SDC PUBLICATIONS	Food Protection Manager
What does FDA stand for?	

SDC PUBLICATIONS	Documents
What does the USDA regulate?	

SDC PUBLICATIONS	72
Who investigates multistate foodborne disease outbreaks?	

SDC PUBLICATIONS	True
Who has the authority to adopt the FDA Food Code and make it law?	

SDC PUBLICATIONS	Records
How often are food establishment inspections performed?	

SDC PUBLICATIONS **One way to demonstrate knowledge is to obtain a** _____ _____ _____ **certificate.**	U.S. Food and Drug Administration
SDC PUBLICATIONS **The inspector is required to _____ their inspection?**	Meat, poultry, and some egg products
SDC PUBLICATIONS **Violations that are "priority items" must be corrected with _____ hours.**	Centers for Disease Control (CDC)
SDC PUBLICATIONS **True or False,** **A corrective action is not meant to be a punishment.**	Local, state, tribal, and federal jurisdictions
SDC PUBLICATIONS **_____ should be kept on all training activities.**	At least every six months